P9-CZV-478

SIMON
PETER

SIMON PETER:
FLAWED BUT FAITHFUL DISCIPLE

Simon Peter: Flawed but Faithful Disciple
978-1-5018-4598-7 Hardcover with jacket
978-1-5018-4599-4 eBook
978-1-5018-4600-7 Large Print

Simon Peter: DVD
978-1-5018-4603-8

Simon Peter: Leader Guide
978-1-5018-4601-4
978-1-5018-4602-1 eBook

Simon Peter: Youth Edition
978-1-5018-4610-6
978-1-5018-4611-3 eBook

Simon Peter: Children's Leader Guide
978-1-5018-4612-0

Also by Adam Hamilton

24 Hours That Changed the World

Christianity and World Religions

Christianity's Family Tree

Confronting the Controversies

Creed

Enough

Faithful

Final Words from the Cross

Forgiveness

Half Truths

John

Leading Beyond the Walls

Love to Stay

Making Sense of the Bible

Moses

Not a Silent Night

Revival

Seeing Gray in a World of Black and White

Selling Swimsuits in the Arctic

Speaking Well

The Call

The Journey

The Way

Unafraid

Unleashing the Word

When Christians Get It Wrong

Why?

For more information, visit www.AdamHamilton.org

ADAM HAMILTON

Author of *The Call* and *Moses*

SIMON PETER

FLAWED BUT FAITHFUL DISCIPLE

Abingdon Press
Nashville

SIMON PETER:
FLAWED BUT FAITHFUL DISCIPLE

Copyright © 2018 Abingdon Press
All rights reserved.

No part of this work may be reproduced or transmitted in any form or by any means, electronic or mechanical, including photocopying and recording, or by any information storage or retrieval system, except as may be expressly permitted by the 1976 Copyright Act or in writing from the publisher. Requests for permission can be addressed to Permissions, The United Methodist Publishing House, 2222 Rosa L. Parks Blvd., Nashville, TN 37228-1306 or e-mailed to permissions@umpublishing.org.

Library of Congress Cataloging-in-Publication data has been requested.

978-1-5018-4598-7

Scripture quotations unless noted otherwise are from the Common English Bible. Copyright © 2011 by the Common English Bible. All rights reserved. Used by permission. www.CommonEnglishBible.com.

Scripture quotations noted NRSV are from the New Revised Standard Version Bible, copyright © 1989 National Council of the Churches of Christ in the United States of America. Used by permission. All rights reserved worldwide. http://nrsvbibles.org/.

Scripture quotations marked (NIV) are taken from the Holy Bible, New International Version®, NIV®. Copyright © 1973, 1978, 1984, 2011 by Biblica, Inc.™ Used by permission of Zondervan. All rights reserved worldwide. www.zondervan.com The "NIV" and "New International Version" are trademarks registered in the United States Patent and Trademark Office by Biblica, Inc™

Scripture quotations noted (KJV) are from The Authorized (King James) Version. Rights in the Authorized Version in the United Kingdom are vested in the Crown. Reproduced by permission of the Crown's patentee, Cambridge University Press.

18 19 20 21 22 23 24 25 26 27 — 10 9 8 7 6 5 4 3 2 1
MANUFACTURED IN THE UNITED STATES OF AMERICA

To Wendell Lady, Chuck Winters, Dennis Wellner,
Dan Entwistle, Brent Messick, Debi Nixon, and Dick Cooper
for your remarkable leadership in building
Resurrection Leawood's permanent sanctuary.

CONTENTS

INTRODUCTION

I've read the Gospels dozens and dozens of times over the last forty years since I first became a follower of Jesus. Most of the time I was focused on Jesus, as the authors of Matthew, Mark, Luke, and John intended. But recently I decided to read through the Gospels paying close attention to Simon Peter. I began to notice just how important a figure he is for each of the Gospel writers. In nearly every episode of Jesus' life and ministry, Peter is somewhere nearby.

Most of the twelve disciples are scarcely mentioned by name in the Gospels. The disciple believed to be the "beloved disciple," John, is mentioned about twenty times by name in the Gospels, as is Judas Iscariot who betrayed Jesus. Andrew, Simon Peter's brother, is mentioned twelve times. Thomas the doubter is mentioned ten times. Bartholomew, James the son of Alphaeus, Simon the Zealot (also known as Simon the Cananaean), and Thaddaeus (also known as Judas son of James) are mentioned only three times each. Simon Peter, on the other hand, is mentioned by name over 120 times.

Peter is not only mentioned more often than the other apostles in the Gospels, he is the leading figure among the twelve in the first half of the Acts of the Apostles. And while

9

Peter and Paul had a bit of a rocky relationship at times (see Galatians 2), Paul recognized Peter, or Cephas as he referred to him, as one of the pillars of the church, entrusted with taking the gospel to the Jews. In addition, two New Testament epistles are attributed to Peter. In the centuries following his death, it was Peter, not Paul, who was considered Rome's first bishop and founding pope.

But what was most fascinating to me as I took a closer look at the Peter stories in the Gospels is that, regardless of the Gospel writer, Peter is nearly always portrayed as a flawed disciple—one who seeks to follow Jesus, yet one who is also confused, afraid, and faltering. So much so that, when his faithfulness mattered most, he denied knowing Jesus.

This stands in contrast to the normal pattern in history where, over time, the less flattering episodes in a beloved figure's life become minimized or forgotten, and only their more heroic acts remembered. The Gospels, all written after the death of Peter, do just the opposite. They each paint him as a flawed follower of Jesus. Why would they do this with the memory of one of their beloved leaders?

I believe the Gospel writers were comfortable telling these stories because Peter himself told these stories again and again across the last thirty years of his life. I suspect Peter highlighted his own failings, using his shortcomings to connect with the common struggles and failings of ordinary followers of Jesus.

My congregation tells me that the most helpful personal stories I share with them are those where I've failed or missed the point. These are the stories my parishioners remember and connect with. In the same way, the stories of Peter's shortcomings serve to humanize Peter, allowing ordinary Christians to identify with him. And in the end, these stories always help to amplify or in some way clarify the identity, power, or mercy of Christ.

While Simon Peter's shortcomings are clearly on display in the Gospels, so also are his courage, his determination, his longing to follow Jesus even if it costs him his life. The early church knew how his story ended after his dramatic denial of Jesus on the night Jesus was arrested. Following Jesus' resurrection and ascension, Peter would, in fact, become the rock upon which the church was built. He would carry his cross to follow Jesus. He would lay down his life for the gospel. While in Peter's flaws Christians might see themselves, they might also see themselves in the moments of Peter's courage and faithfulness, and ultimately they might see in him a picture of what they might aspire to be when empowered and led by the Spirit.

This book, like most of my books, is not intended to be a scholarly treatise. I love reading the works of scholars and have done so in preparing this work. I hope to offer some of the information you would discover if you were reading a scholarly work on Peter. I'll include maps, photos, and historical background along with some of the other exegetical insights of biblical scholars. This book is also not a comprehensive biography of Peter. I've left many episodes from Peter's story on the proverbial cutting room floor and instead will focus on six of the best-known stories from Peter's life. These stories were preserved in the kerygma of the early church—its preaching—and as such they became a vehicle through which the gospel of Jesus Christ was preached and by means of which believers heard the Word of God. My hope is to give you a sense of the man, Peter, and to invite you to understand how Peter's story speaks to us today, how these stories serve as God's Word to us, helping us both to know Christ more fully and to become the disciples Christ calls us to be. In this sense the book is part scholarly work, part sermon, and part devotional.

Ultimately, I hope to help you see yourself in Simon Peter, the flawed but ultimately faithful follower of Jesus Christ. With that in mind, let's begin our study.

1

THE CALL OF THE FISHERMAN

One day Jesus was standing beside Lake Gennesaret when the crowd pressed in around him to hear God's word. Jesus saw two boats sitting by the lake. The fishermen had gone ashore and were washing their nets. Jesus boarded one of the boats, the one that belonged to Simon, then asked him to row out a little distance from the shore. Jesus sat down and taught the crowds from the boat. When he finished speaking to the crowds, he said to Simon, "Row out farther, into the deep water, and drop your nets for a catch."

Simon replied, "Master, we've worked hard all night and caught nothing. But because you say so, I'll drop the nets."

So they dropped the nets and their catch was so huge that their nets were splitting. They signaled for their partners in the other boat to come and help them. They filled both boats so full that they were about to sink. When Simon Peter saw the catch, he fell at Jesus' knees and said, "Leave me, Lord, for I'm a sinner!" Peter and those with him were overcome with amazement because of the number of fish they caught. James and John, Zebedee's sons, were Simon's partners and they were amazed too.

Jesus said to Simon, "Don't be afraid. From now on, you will be fishing for people." As soon as they brought the boats to the shore, they left everything and followed Jesus.

(Luke 5:1-11)

Matthew, Mark, Luke, and John, composing their Gospels in the second half of the first century, each sought to lead their readers to faith, or to a deeper faith, in Jesus Christ. In literary terms, Jesus is the protagonist of the Gospels—the heroic central figure around whom the entire story, and I would add the Christian faith, revolves. He came to draw the world to God, and to reveal God to the world.

While Jesus is the protagonist of the Gospels, in each of them Simon Peter serves, to borrow another literary term, as a "foil" to Jesus. A foil is a supporting character whose part contrasts, highlights, and even exalts the qualities of the lead character. Often it is the foil's *shortcomings* and *missteps* that magnify the protagonist's virtues. In the case of Simon Peter, the Gospel writers portray bumbling, fumbling, and stumbling again and again. Each time, Peter's blunder serves to reveal some dimension of Jesus' character or to make clear some aspect of Christ's message.

But Simon Peter's role is not only as foil to Jesus. The Gospel writers also lift up Simon Peter as representing those of us who believe in and seek to follow Jesus. Like Peter, you and I have chosen to follow Jesus. We've given up something to answer his call. At our best we would, like Peter, boldly proclaim that we would die for Christ if necessary. Yet we've all at times lost our courage, taken our eyes off of Jesus, misunderstood his teaching, and even denied him. Just as Jesus reveals and represents God, Simon Peter represents all who seek to follow Jesus.

What is amazing about the Gospels' portrayal of Simon Peter is that Matthew, Mark, Luke, and John let us see Peter's missteps, even highlight them. Peter was, after all, the leader of the Twelve. His leadership of the early church was profound. And, by the time the Gospels were written, he'd been put to death by the Romans for his faith in Christ. It would have been understandable if they had sanitized his story, as we do in the eulogies of our loved ones, telling only the good and lovely things about them and leaving off their list of shortcomings. But instead, each of the Gospels allows us to see Simon Peter "warts and all." As I noted in the introduction, I believe they did this because Peter himself must have done this in his preaching across the thirty-plus years between Jesus' death and his own. It was this that gave Simon Peter's preaching such power— his ability to tell of his shortcomings in a way that connected with ordinary believers, which in turn magnified the Christ he proclaimed.

Peter was a flawed, yet ultimately faithful, disciple.

There is much that is unknown about Simon Peter's background, but I'd like to explore what little we do know about Simon's early life as a fisherman on the Sea of Galilee before we begin to explore the story of his initial encounter with Jesus.

The Sea of Galilee

It's quite a stretch to call the Sea of Galilee, also called the Kinneret Lake, a "sea." Thirteen miles from north to south, and eight miles east to west at its widest, it is a modest-sized lake

Top: A view from the Sea of Galilee looking toward (from left to right): Mount Arbel, Magdala, and Ginosaur.

Center: Sunrise over the Sea of Galilee.

Bottom: From Tabgha on the north shore of the Sea of Galilee, looking south as the sun was preparing to set.

compared with many others. But this lake has always played a critical role in the lives of those who have lived in the Holy Land over the millennia that human beings have inhabited this area.

The lake is beautiful, surrounded by dormant volcanoes that rise as high as 1,600 feet from its banks. Sitting 700 feet *below* sea level, it is the lowest freshwater body in the world and the second lowest lake on earth, after the Dead Sea ninety miles to the south.

Surprising to most who visit the Holy Land, there is very little development along the shores of the sea today. Tiberias is the largest city; located on the western shore of the lake, it has a population of about forty-five thousand people. There are a number of much smaller communities dotting the shoreline, but by and large, the lake looks as it did two thousand years ago when a handful of small fishing villages dotted the lakeshore.

In the time of Christ, an imaginary dividing line separated the eastern and western sides of the lake. That line began from the point the Jordan River entered the Sea of Galilee to the north, and extended to where it exited the sea to the south. West of the Jordan River, the region was called Galilee. The fishing villages on that side of the lake, as well as the land continuing for another eighteen miles to the west, were governed by Herod Antipas, son of Herod the Great. The eastern part of the lake and the land beyond—Gaulanitis, Trachonitus, Batanea, and Auranitis—was ruled by Antipas's half-brother, Herod Philip. (Our modern word, *Golan*, comes from the ancient Gaulanitis, and Gaulanitis consisted of much of the area we call the Golan Heights today).

Simon Peter's story begins along the lakeshore, just east of the Jordan River, in Gaulanitis, in a town called Bethsaida.

John's Gospel tells us that Simon and his brother Andrew (along with their friend Philip) were from a village called Bethsaida—the town's name means "house of hunters," or more likely, "house of fishermen." There are two different archaeological sites that could be ancient Bethsaida, just a few

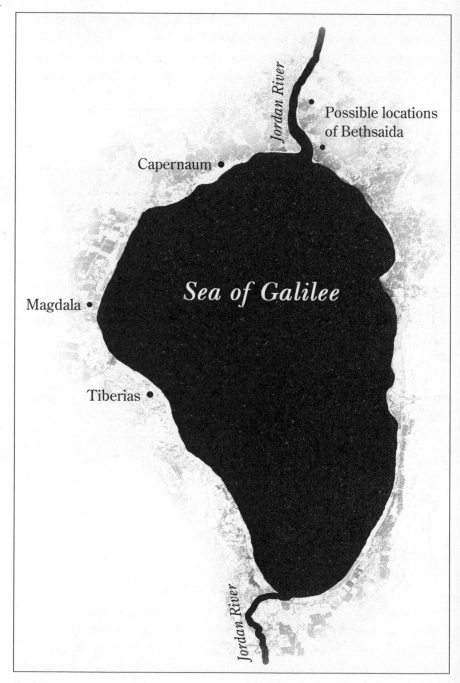

Jordan River

Possible locations
of Bethsaida

Capernaum •

Magdala •

Sea of Galilee

Tiberias •

Jordan River

miles apart. Both are just north of the Sea of Galilee and just east of the Jordan River as it enters the Sea of Galilee. This would have placed Bethsaida just barely inside Herod Philip's domain, while just a few yards away, on the west bank of the Jordan, was Galilee ruled over by Philip's half-brother Herod Antipas.

If you were to visit the Holy Land and you sought to visit Simon's hometown, you'd likely be taken to an archaeological site named Et-Tell. It is located about a mile and a half north of the current coastline of the Sea of Galilee, and again, just east of the Jordan. Some who believe this is the biblical Bethsaida suggest that the shoreline of the Sea of Galilee was much closer to this village two thousand years ago. Walking around the site, you will see the excavated foundations of several large ancient homes, including one called "the Fisherman's home" because weights and hooks used in fishing have been discovered there. You'll also see the "Winemaker's home" where archaeologists discovered an undisturbed ancient wine cellar. You can also imagine, as you look to the north and west, an area where Jesus was said to have fed the five thousand (Luke 9:10-17), or picture Jesus healing the blind man just outside of town (Mark 8:22-25).

A second possible site for Bethsaida, el-Araj, is closer to the Sea of Galilee—so close in fact that the location has, throughout history, often been underwater. On my last visit to the area, I attempted to visit the archaeological site but could not get to it because of the mud. It appears to many a better location for the fishing village of Simon and his brother, but the jury is still out on which of these locations, if either, is Bethsaida where Simon and his brother Andrew would have grown up.

Simon Bar Jonah

Peter's given name at birth was Simon, or Simeon as it appears twice in the New Testament. Yet the biblical names have usually been anglicized in our English translations. In the Aramaic spoken in Galilee in the first century, he would likely have been called Shimon. Shimon is related to the Hebrew word *shema*, which means "to hear" or "to listen." It was a very common name in first-century Judaism, with nine different Simons or Shimons mentioned in the New Testament. Two of the twelve disciples bear this name. A sibling of Jesus, too, is named Simon.

The name was popularized by the events Jews celebrate in the festival of Hanukkah. In 167 BC, a band of brothers, priests, and warriors popularly called the Maccabees, led by their father, Mattathias, revolted against the Seleucid Empire. The Seleucid king, Antiochus IV, ruling from Damascus, sought to force Greek customs, religion, and culture on the Jewish people, going so far as to have a pig sacrificed to Zeus in the temple in Jerusalem. The Jewish rebels won a surprising victory over the far more powerful Seleucids, and were able to rededicate the temple in 164 BC. Simon the Maccabee, one of the warrior sons, eventually ruled as high priest and king. A century and a half later, parents were still naming their children after him, perhaps in the hope that their sons, like Simon Maccabee, might help overthrow their Roman overseers and once again see a free Israel.*

Jewish naming conventions typically identified a man by both his given name and his father's name. In Matthew, Jesus addresses Simon as "Simon son of Jonah" (Simon bar Jonah), though in John's Gospel he is referred to as "Simon son of John."† There's something delightful about imagining Simon's father, no doubt a fisherman, being named after the biblical Jonah, who spent three days in the belly of a big fish.

Simon's and Andrew's earliest experience fishing was likely as little boys, taken by Jonah to fish using fishing line and hook cast from the shores of the lake or the banks of the Jordan River.

---

* You can read more about this in 1 Maccabees, a fascinating read about these events.

† Various reasons are sometimes given for these two different names and how they might be reconciled, but some scholars are content to note they are audibly similar, which may explain how Matthew's Gospel reflected one name and John's another.

I imagine these boys learning about fishing, life, and faith from their father. Jimmy Carter once said, "Many of the most highly publicized events of my presidency are not nearly as memorable or significant in my life as fishing with my daddy."[1] I imagine something similar was true for Simon and Andrew. This was how Jewish boys grew up and learned to be men.

Later, when they were strong and tall enough to handle the casting nets, they would have learned to cast these nets from the shore or from small boats. These nets were capable of catching dozens of fish at a time. In early adolescence, they would have joined the other men on the fishing boats, using dragnets or trammel nets to haul in much larger quantities of fish.

Fishermen in the Greco-Roman World

Before we finally consider Simon's first encounters with Jesus, let's explore one last bit of background information that might help us know Simon: the socioeconomic place that fishermen and fishmongers occupied in first-century Judaism and in the broader ancient world.

Among the Jewish population there was a class of people, going back hundreds of years before the time of Jesus and Peter, called *am ha'aretz*. The phrase literally means, "people of the land." The term has an interesting history, but by the time of Simon Peter it meant people who were poor, uneducated, lower class, and particularly people who were not careful in their observance of the Law.

The Galilee region was known for being home to, and surrounded by, large numbers of Gentiles. It was supposed by some Jews that this fact led Jews in Galilee to be less stringent in their observance of the Law. The fishermen who made their living on the shoreline of the lake were among the *am ha'aretz*. There were no doubt exceptions, but generally they were seen as less educated, being lower income, and less devout in their keeping of the Law.

In the Book of Acts, the religious leaders in Jerusalem viewed Simon and the other disciples as "unlearned" or, more literally, "those who could not write." They were surprised when Peter spoke with such eloquence and power about the gospel of Jesus.

While some of the Jewish religious leaders considered Peter and his companions to be *am ha'aretz*, others would have looked down upon these Galilean fisherman for different reasons.

Fish was a food staple throughout the Roman Empire. Few people could afford beef or even lamb, but they could afford fish. Wealthy people ate fresh fish, which they typically grilled; most others ate salted, pickled, or dried fish. As in modern times, people of the ancient world routinely complained about the price of staples, including fish. That led them, at times, to grouse about fishermen and fishmongers. At least one ancient source described fishmongers as "murderous, wealthy thieves."[2] By association, fishermen were sometimes denounced as well.

In contrast, Jesus came to the Sea of Galilee from Nazareth and made the shoreline communities of the lake the focus and home base of his ministry. He called the *am ha'aretz*, including fishermen, to be his disciples. Most of his ministry was devoted to these multitudes. And his response to the religious leaders who looked down upon the *am ha'aretz* was: "Woe unto you, scribes and Pharisees, hypocrites!" (Matthew 23:13 KJV).

As we prepare to dive into Simon's earliest encounters with Jesus, and to make sense of Peter's call story, allow me to remind you of the three most common ways of fishing on the Sea of Galilee.

Line and hook were not uncommon methods for fishing in New Testament times. At least once in the Gospels, Jesus instructs Peter to cast a line with a hook in order to catch a fish (Matthew 17:24-27), promising that the first fish Peter catches will have a coin in its mouth that Peter should use to pay the temple tax for them both. While someone might catch a single fish this way from time to time, catching one fish at a time was not profitable.

Two fishermen preparing to fish by dragnet at sunset on the Sea of Galilee. The city of Tiberias is in the background.

2. We also know that fishermen on the Sea of Galilee threw casting nets, often from the shoreline. This method of fishing is still used to this day, and it is this form of fishing that you'll often see illustrated by fishermen on the boats that take tourists and pilgrims across the Sea of Galilee. If you've never seen anyone cast nets for fish, you might enjoy watching a young guy who calls himself the "Fish Whisperer." Google him and you'll find his videos on YouTube, including one where he uses a casting net to bring in a huge haul of fish.*

3. But the method most often used by crews of professional fishermen in the first century was called dragnet or seine fishing. In this type of fishing, two boats might work together, lowering a large net into the water, fishermen in each boat holding on to one end of the net. The boats would row forward, spreading apart some distance and catching large numbers of a variety of fish in the nets, then the boats would come together and the nets, hopefully filled with fish, would be hauled into one boat or the other.

Both casting nets and seine nets require brute strength when hauling in the fish. It is not hard to imagine the calloused

---

* See this at: https://www.youtube.com/watch?v=NOSGMrBwN1w. This is, of course, not the same as the dragnet technique the disciples deployed most often, but it gives you a glimpse of net fishing.

hands and the strong arms of the men who made their living in this way.

With all of this background in mind, we're ready to explore the Gospel stories involving Simon, starting with his first-time encounter with Jesus, as well as a subsequent encounter at which time Simon answered Jesus' call to join him in order to "fish for people."

From Simon to Peter

We often think that the first encounter Simon had with Jesus was on the seashore of the Sea of Galilee. But John's Gospel tells us they first met months earlier. Jesus grew up in Nazareth, about sixteen miles due west of the southern tip of the Sea of Galilee. But at the age of thirty, he traveled sixty miles southeast, as the

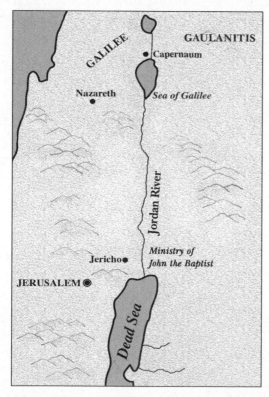

crow flies, to a place along the Jordan River, just before it flows into the Dead Sea, where his cousin John the Baptist was preaching and baptizing. John refers to this as "Bethany beyond the Jordan." No one knows where this site is. But the story is remembered both in Jordan and Israel at a place east of Jericho, where, on both banks of the Jordan, pilgrims now step into the muddy water of the Jordan to recall their baptism. Here's how Luke describes John's ministry: "John went throughout the region of the Jordan River, calling for people to be baptized to show that they were changing their hearts and lives and wanted God to forgive their sins" (Luke 3:3).

Jesus was not the only one who came from Galilee to hear John preach. Andrew, Philip, Nathaniel, and Simon had also come to hear John. What was it that led these Galilean fishermen, who, it was supposed, were not so religiously devout, to take a week away from their nets and livelihood, traveling four or five days on foot each way, to hear John preaching in the desert? Was it a yearning for forgiveness? A desire to find a deeper faith? A sense that they had strayed from God's path? Or a conviction that God's kingdom, and the coming of the Messiah, were drawing near?

The arrival of Jesus as well as Philip, Andrew, Simon, and Nathanael tells us that word of John's ministry had spread to Galilee and that there were likely many who felt an inner compulsion to come to hear John, to be baptized by him as an expression of their desire to repent, and to offer their lives to God. Listen to how the Gospel of John describes the first encounter between Jesus, Andrew, and Simon:

> *John was standing again with two of his disciples.*
> *When he saw Jesus walking along he said, "Look! The*
> *Lamb of God!" The two disciples heard what he said,*
> *and they followed Jesus.*
>
> *When Jesus turned and saw them following, he asked,*
> *"What are you looking for?"*
>
> *They said, "Rabbi (which is translated* Teacher*),*
> *where are you staying?"*
>
> *He replied, "Come and see." So they went and saw*
> *where he was staying, and they remained with him*
> *that day. It was about four o'clock in the afternoon.*

> *One of the two disciples who heard what John said and followed Jesus was Andrew, the brother of Simon Peter. He first found his own brother Simon and said to him, "We have found the Messiah" (which is translated Christ). He led him to Jesus.*
>
> *(John 1:35-42a)*

It is Andrew who leads his brother Simon to meet Jesus, whom Andrew identifies as the Messiah (a title that signifies God's chosen king).

I love this picture on two fronts. The first is the invitation it gives us to share our faith with our siblings. I have two sisters and two brothers. I love them and regularly pray for them. In recent years, it has been a joy to see my siblings all on a journey to know who Jesus is and to seek to follow him. Andrew becomes a picture for us of drawing our siblings to Christ. The second thing that is compelling about Andrew is that, once Simon came to faith, Andrew took a backseat role to Simon, and Andrew seemed okay with that. In the handful of times Andrew is mentioned in the Gospels, he is always playing a supportive role, never in the limelight. He becomes the patron saint of those who work behind the scenes, leading people to faith and encouraging and helping them to serve.

John goes on to tell us what happened on that first encounter between Jesus and Simon: "Jesus looked at him and said, 'You are Simon, son of John. You will be called Cephas' (which is translated *Peter*)" (John 1:42). Cephas (pronounced Kay-fus) in Aramaic is Petros or Peter in Greek. Both words mean Rock.

Many of us give nicknames to our friends; maybe your friends have bestowed one upon you. Nicknames usually reveal something about us, or at least about how people perceive us. They are often a sign of affection. We know that Jesus called James and John, Simon's fishing partners, the "Sons of Thunder." I love that nickname—it sounds downright *bad*. But it was Simon's nickname that took the cake. Long before actor

26

and World Wrestling Federation wrestler Dwayne Johnson christened himself "The Rock," Jesus gave Simon this name. Simon was "the Rock."*

Why did Jesus choose this nickname for Simon? Was it because he was strong and mighty, giant biceps forged from hauling in fishing nets? Possibly. Or could there be something else? Throughout the Hebrew Bible, God is described as a Rock, or *the* Rock. God is steady, strong, immovable, like a rock. But how could Jesus call Simon a rock? After all, this man is going to blow it consistently. He will be less like a rock and more like a reed or blade of grass, easily moved, swayed, or broken. He will miss the point again and again. Why in the world would Jesus call him "the Rock"? I think it's because Jesus saw past the unsteady, easily unnerved man Simon was. He could see what Simon one day would become: immovable, foundational, steady, strong. Jesus could see that one day the Rock would live into this auspicious name.

The nickname stuck, a term of endearment and a name meant to encourage Simon. In the Gospels the name Simon appears 54 times in reference to Simon Peter, but "Rock" (Peter) is used 115 times.

Catholics used to observe the tradition of young people adopting the name of a saint at confirmation. My father's given name was Everett, but at confirmation he chose the name Mark, after St. Mark the Gospel writer. My dad has gone by this name ever since (only his mother got away with continuing to call him Everett!). In the case of Simon, Jesus didn't give him the name of a person he hoped Simon would emulate. Instead, Jesus gave him a vision of what he might be—that one day he'd be a rock for others.

---

* Some have suggested that Simon already had the nickname Rock and that Jesus was simply recognizing and affirming that one day Simon would live up to this nickname. I think the simplest reading of the Gospel is that Jesus is here giving this name to Simon.

27

If Jesus were to give you a nickname describing the potential he saw in you, not the person you are but the person you could become, what nickname would you hope he might choose for you? Beautiful? Selfless? Courageous? Bold? Servant? Loving? I'd want him to call me "Faithful," not because I am a faithful disciple, but because that is what I long to be.

After this initial encounter between Jesus and Simon Peter, Jesus headed into the wilderness of Judea—a desert-like area near the site where John was baptizing. He went to fast and to seek God, and there he was tempted and tested. Meanwhile Simon, Andrew, Philip, and Nathanael returned to Galilee, to their everyday lives, having renewed their commitment to God. I suspect they were also quite curious about this man, Jesus, whom they had just met.

A month and a half went by following Peter's first encounter with Jesus. He'd returned to his fishing business with his brother and the sons of Zebedee, James and John. And while Simon and Andrew had grown up in Bethsaida, as adult men they now lived in the town of Capernaum, four miles west of Bethsaida, a town also located on the north shore of the Sea of Galilee.

Simon had married, likely when he was fourteen to sixteen years of age. His wife was from Capernaum, and the young couple likely had moved into living quarters that had been added to the home she'd grown up in. Capernaum was in Galilee proper, and the taxes in Galilee were lower than those in Gaulanitis, which provided an incentive to live in the hometown of Simon's wife rather than in Bethsaida.

Run by the Franciscans, the archaeological site of Capernaum is one of my favorite places in all of the Holy Land. Walking on the excavated remains of the city, you know you are walking where Peter walked, in the town where he and his family lived, and in the place where so many Gospel stories took place. We do not always know whether Jesus was here or there when we traverse the Holy Land, but Capernaum became Jesus' hometown during his three years of public ministry, with Jesus apparently living in the home of Simon Peter's mother-in-law where Peter himself lived. If you are walking anywhere in Capernaum, you are likely walking where Jesus walked.

A visit to Capernaum will take you to a large modern church that looks like a spaceship, built atop and hovering over the ruins of an ancient church. Beneath the church are the ruins of an old house that was expanded a couple of times. This home, it is believed, was the home of Simon, his wife, her mother, and Jesus himself when he was staying in Capernaum. (Matthew 4 notes that Jesus settled in Capernaum, and in Matthew 9:1 it is referred to as Jesus' "own city.")

The village was home to as many as 1,500 people by some estimates. It was located very near if not actually on a major trade route linking Egypt to Damascus, which then went on to the major cities to the east—a road often referred to as the Via Maris (Way of the Sea) or the International Trunk Road. From the most ancient of times, this road conveyed trade and travelers from Africa to Asia. A mile marker for this trade route can be seen among the stones at Capernaum. This strategic location

In 1990 the Franciscans built the Church of St. Peter over the ruins of what are believed to be the first-century home of Simon Peter, where Jesus lived as Peter's guest when he was in Capernaum. In the foreground you can see the foundation walls of some of the homes in ancient Capernaum built of black basalt stone.

29

The foundation walls of an octagonal shaped church built in the 400s in Capernaum, atop an earlier house church, atop the original ruins of a first-century home believed to be that of Simon Peter. Above these ruins are the modern Church of St. Peter.

made it an important place for fishermen to sell their wares to the caravans of people passing through.

It was to this village that Jesus came, after having been rejected in his own hometown of Nazareth. There he began to teach, to preach, and to heal. And it was here that he called Simon to follow him.

Borrowing Simon's Boat:
Our Time, Talent, and Stuff

One morning as Jesus was teaching along the shoreline near Capernaum, large crowds began to press in upon him. But four fishermen, Simon and Andrew, James and John, were also standing nearby along with their hired men. They'd just come in from fishing all night, and they were cleaning and mending their nets.

You might ask why they had been fishing at night. If you are fishing with line and lure, you want the fish to see the lure, so you fish during the day. But if you are using a dragnet, pulled behind two boats to haul in entire schools of fish, you fish at night so the fish can't see the nets. I've seen this kind of fishing on multiple occasions. Typically I've seen two small fishing boats, piles of nets inside, departing for areas just off the shore. I've seen the fisherman light a lamp and set it on a float in the middle of the water. This attracts fish. Then they circle around with each boat holding on to one side of the net. They drop the net, which is weighted at the bottom, and then power their boats to encircle what they hope will be schools of fish drawn toward the light.

On the particular night before Jesus called Simon Peter, the brothers and their hired hands had caught nothing. If you enjoy fishing as a hobby, you surely have had the same experience on occasion. It's pretty common to go out and come back empty-handed. But your next meal, much less your family's income, probably didn't depend on whether you caught a fish.

For Peter, Andrew, James, and John, fishing was their livelihood, and they'd had a bad night. They were no doubt tired and discouraged and ready to go home. But first they had to clean their nets. This was important: if nets are put away dirty or wet, they rot. No one who makes a livelihood from fishing can afford that.

On that day, though it was early morning, Jesus already had a large crowd pressing in around him to hear his message. Just then, Jesus saw two boats sitting by the lake while the fishermen were washing their nets (or, more likely, Jesus planned to show up teaching at precisely this place and time, knowing Peter and Andrew, James and John would be there). Jesus boarded one of the boats, the one that belonged to Simon, then asked him to row out a little distance from the shore. When Simon did this, Jesus sat down and taught the crowds from the boat (Luke 5:1-3).

Jesus could actually preach more effectively to these people from the boat. He wouldn't be crushed by the crowds that had been pressing in on him at the shoreline. More people could see him. And as you may have noticed if you've been on the water forty or fifty yards from shore, people on the shore can hear you perfectly because the water acts as a sounding board.

But Jesus' strategy was about more than finding the best spot to preach. He wanted to invite Simon Peter's help. Most of us don't want people helping us, but we're open to helping someone else. Jesus was appealing to that instinct. Often the best way to build a relationship with people is to ask for their help: "Can I borrow a cup of sugar?" "Could you lend me a hand?" I think Jesus was looking for a way to draw Peter into his movement. So he asked to borrow Peter's boat.

Perhaps Jesus also wanted Peter as a captive audience. If Peter rowed out with Jesus, he would literally be stuck listening to Jesus' message. He couldn't even fall asleep because all the eyes on the shore would be focused his way.

Imagine how Simon felt that morning, after fishing all night long and catching nothing, when Jesus stepped into his boat and asked him to push off the shoreline. Jesus asked Simon to do something he undoubtedly didn't want to do, yet Simon did it anyway.

Has anyone ever asked you to do something, and you really didn't want to do it because it was an inconvenience? Perhaps you were tired—and yet you did it anyway? Here's what Peter would learn again and again: *Jesus routinely inconveniences his followers.*

He asks us to give our time, and sometimes to borrow our stuff, in order to accomplish his work. He likes to use our skills, our abilities, whatever is at our disposal that we can offer. But Jesus doesn't always ask for our help in the way he called on Peter. Sometimes his call is in the form of a bulletin announcement at church or a sermon in which an invitation is given or maybe we're reading the Bible or praying, and we feel a nudge from the Spirit. Often it is a person in need who presents the opportunity—we see someone in need and feel Christ tugging on our heart. Our task is to pay attention to what's happening around us and to tune our hearts to hear his call.

Even though it's Jesus who asks for our help, and even though we seek to be Christ's followers, we will often feel reluctant and hesitant. We make excuses. We may find ourselves responding, "Jesus, I'm really busy and I have a million other things I need to do. Could you please find someone else?" Peter had a great excuse: "Lord, I've been fishing all night and I'm so tired." But Peter didn't say that. He simply got in the boat. There's a lesson in that for us.

Jesus showed up at church one Sunday recently, in the form of a homeless woman who needed a hand. A couple in the church had picked her up after worship, offering to give her a lift, but did not realize what that would entail. As they spoke to her, they saw that she would need more than a lift; she would need a hotel room for the night until she could get help in the morning. The couple had lunch plans and places to go, but in that moment they changed their plans. They made arrangements to get her settled for the day and assisted her in finding help in the morning. Jesus showed up in an inconvenient way, but like Peter, they said "yes, Lord." Jesus borrowed their SUV and some of their money and time that day.

Often Jesus asks to borrow our passion or skills to use it for his purposes. Jason loves cars, and he's great at fixing them. Jesus asked to borrow his skills and passion in order to start a ministry to help people with limited finances to repair their cars when otherwise they could not afford it. This includes single moms, struggling families, and a host of others. Jesus even asked to borrow some of Jason's money to purchase a car repair shop that would serve as a regular business during the day, but a place for volunteers to come and repair cars in the evenings.

Mary spent her life as a guidance counselor at a local college. She's a natural problem solver. When she retired, Jesus asked to borrow some of her newfound time in order to help in our congregational care ministry, visiting with and caring for people who were in need of guidance, love, and care. It's not how she envisioned spending her retirement, but it has given her far more joy than she ever imagined as she serves Jesus by serving others.

I wonder what your boat, nets, and skills are that Jesus might call you to use in service for him and to or with others?

Put Out into the Deep Water and Throw Out the Net

Let's see what happened after Jesus finished preaching from Peter's boat: "When he finished speaking to the crowds, he said to Simon, 'Row out farther, into the deep water, and drop your nets for a catch.'" Simon hesitated and replied, "Master, we've worked hard all night and caught nothing" (Luke 5:4-5) By this time the nets were cleaned and dry. The men were ready for bed. And didn't Jesus know that net fishing isn't good during the day? I can imagine Peter leaving a pregnant pause, hoping Jesus would say, "No worries, Simon. I understand, you are tired and you've just cleaned the nets. Listen, we'll do this another time." But Jesus didn't say that. It was surely an uncomfortable few moments. Then finally, in the heavy silence, Peter spoke up: "But because you say so, I'll drop the nets."

The words *"because you say so"* reflect Simon Peter's *reluctant obedience*. Perhaps you can relate to Simon's reluctant obedience. There are times when Jesus asks us to do things that we don't want to do, when we feel tired, or when what we're being asked to do seems to make no sense to us. I have, on many occasions, been a very *reluctant disciple*. For us, the deep water is the place where Jesus calls us to go when we'd rather stay on the shore. We feel Christ calling and we drag our feet, and sometimes we even say no.

Overcoming Our Excuses

As a pastor, I have often found myself making excuses. In fact, I feel like I have this conversation with Jesus every week. I say, "Lord, I'm tired, I don't want to, please find someone else." And then I am reminded of Peter's words, "Lord, because you say so, I will do it." When I ultimately do what I feel Jesus nudging me to do, even if I do it begrudgingly, I usually find myself in the midst of the most meaningful events.

John Lennon famously sang, "Life is what happens to you while you're busy making other plans." It's true with Jesus too. So often, the most important things in our lives happen when Jesus interrupts what we're doing with a nudge and says, "I need you to..." and, reluctantly, we go.

It happened to me the week I was studying this very Scripture from Luke, preparing a sermon on this text. I'd already put in sixty hours at work that week and it wasn't yet Sunday. I was on my way home, where a long list of chores awaited, when I got a call from a member who told me her friend was dying. She asked if I could stop by to see her. My first thought was: We have an entire pastoral care team, can I send one of them? That may have been the right answer in another situation, but I felt a nudge, as if Jesus were saying I was to go to see the dying woman myself. Reluctantly, almost begrudgingly, I prayed Simon Peter's words, "Because you say so, I'll drop the nets." That night I spent an hour with the dying woman and her husband in their home. We had a deeply moving conversation—one that was comforting and hopeful and left both the couple and me filled with gratitude and joy, even in the face of her impending death. Though I went reluctantly, I found that I was the one who was blessed by this encounter.

I had the same experience on a recent mission trip to Honduras, providing leadership training and helping with construction on a school. I'd been there four other times and always found it a blessing, but I'll be honest: As the date approached for the Honduras trip, I was thinking to myself, Why did I agree to do this? I had multiple projects at the church that needed my attention and a book manuscript that was past due and a host of things that needed my time around the house. For these reasons, I was actually dreading the trip.

LaVon, my wife, was going with me, and for that I was grateful, but as we boarded the plane, I continued to feel like the reluctant disciple with nothing left to give.

We were going to visit the church and school that members of Church of the Resurrection had built in Ciudad España. The village received its name because it was constructed by the Spanish Red Cross in the wake of Hurricane Mitch in 1998. Mitch had poured down disaster upon this small Central American country, leaving seven thousand dead and over a million people homeless in Honduras alone. When I first visited this community in 2003, we found a United Methodist congregation that was meeting under a tree. We dreamed of a church building and school that would positively affect the entire community. Our members, alongside Hondurans, helped built these facilities during trips between 2005 and 2007. Then we added a high school in 2015. Hundreds of us had gone to Ciudad España to work over the years. Most were at least somewhat reluctant as they went, but all said, "Lord, because you say so, I will go."

When our team arrived at the school, with me as a reluctant participant, the students were lining the drive to the school to welcome us: 377 children gathered to greet us. I was awestruck to see them, and moved to tears. Over the next few days I had the chance to teach, to do a little construction work, and to listen to the stories of these children and their families. As we left, I thought of Simon Peter, Andrew, James, and John as they reluctantly let down their nets one more time because Jesus asked them to. Looking back at the Juan Wesley School as we drove away, I felt I'd witnessed the kind of miracle those first apostles experienced that day on the Sea of Galilee. That night I turned to LaVon and said, "My soul needed this." She whispered, "Mine too." But we almost missed it with a thousand excellent excuses.

Simon Peter and his colleagues might well have missed a miraculous blessing had Peter not said, "But because you say so..."

A Huge Haul of Fish

Instead of making excuses in response to Jesus' invitation, Peter beckoned to his brother, Andrew, and their two hired hands to bring the newly cleaned nets, get back in the boat, and row out to deep water.

Luke tells us that when Simon and Andrew and their friends reached the spot Jesus had suggested, "They dropped the nets and their catch was so huge that their nets were splitting." They signaled for their friends James and John to hurry to come in the other boat and help them. They filled both boats so full that they were about to sink.

What a haul of fish! Simon fell to his knees right then in the boat and exclaimed, "Leave me, Lord, for I'm a sinner!" He was frightened and awestruck. Peter's response reminds me of Isaiah's response to his vision of seeing God's glory. He cried out, "Woe is me! I am lost, for I am a man of unclean lips, and I live among a people of unclean lips; yet my eyes have seen the King, the LORD of hosts!" (Isaiah 6:5 NRSV). Peter's response reflects what the Bible describes as the "fear of the Lord"—a reverence, awe, and sense of unworthiness.

This is what Peter felt witnessed this dramatic miracle. It is what I felt as I looked at those 377 children at the Juan Wesley School in Honduras—a catch of "fish" the likes of which I had never imagined possible.

Pay particular attention to Jesus' response to Simon's words: "Don't be afraid. From now on, you will be fishing for people."

The first part of Jesus' call was simply not to be fearful. Have you ever noticed how many times *that* message occurs in the Gospels? Many of the things that Jesus calls us to do leave us feeling a bit afraid. For me, that included answering the call to full-time ministry and starting a church, but it was also getting married, having children, caring for people I don't know, going to places I've never been, giving money I didn't think I could spare. In a thousand ways he's had to reassure me with the words, "Don't be afraid" before he called me to his mission in the moment, for the day, in my life.

Jesus called upon Peter to leave his fishing business behind and to join him in the mission to fish for people. By the way, when you hear someone saying, "Don't be afraid," there's a good chance you should be a bit worried—the journey you are being invited to take likely comes with some risk, or else the warning wouldn't be needed. But when it is Jesus who gives the invitation, you know that somehow, you don't have to be afraid.

Fishing for People

I love this metaphor for Jesus' mission—fishing for people. It is drawing people into the Kingdom dragnet, drawing them to God, leading them to become a part of the kingdom of God. But Jesus' followers are not the only ones fishing for people.

I recently saw an interview with a white nationalist who wants to make America an exclusively white nation and send other people packing. He said, "equality is for losers." As a neo-Nazi, he's fishing for people too. He's trying to go to college campuses and recruit young people to think like he does and to be a part of a world that operates according to his values.

The movement Jesus started couldn't be more different. He invites people to join him in loving God with all their hearts and to love their neighbors around them just as they love them-selves. He beckons us to love even our enemies. The movement Jesus started would aim to transform the world; to pray for, and work to God's kingdom to come, and God's will to be done, on earth as it is in heaven.

"Go out and fish for people and show them how much they matter to you and to God," Jesus says. "Offer them forgiveness, redemption, new life, and hope." If you are a Christian, you are a part of this movement. Have you ever stopped to think about what that word implies? It suggests something that is always moving, not sitting still—always reaching out in love, always fishing for people. Are you sitting still and asking God to use someone else, or are you part of a movement?

Jesus still calls us to follow and to fish. Each morning when you wake up, if you are in his movement, I encourage you to pray some variation of this prayer, "Here I am, Lord. Everything I have is yours. Send me on your mission today. Help me fish for people." Each day, we're called to draw people to Christ— to influence them positively and to help them see his love and grace through us. If you're reading this book as part of a study for a Sunday school class or another group at church, you're there because someone drew you to Christ. Your calling is to draw others to be part of his movement.

That day at the lakeshore, Jesus borrowed Simon Peter's boat, then gave him a glimpse of what could happen if he went out to the deep water and let down his nets. But the most important thing that happened that day happened when Jesus called Simon to leave behind his nets and to join the mission to fish for people.

Christ is calling you to follow him. He's asking to use you and your boat. It's okay if you are, at times, a bit reluctant. Most of the people God called in Scripture were a bit reticent too. But in the end, the adventure begins when we say, Yes! And that yes is to a mission of fishing for people.

How are you influencing people for Christ? How do you represent him by your actions and by your words?

Here's how the story of Peter's call ends: "As soon as they brought the boats to the shore, they left everything and followed Jesus." This is where Simon Peter's real adventure begins. And this is where our adventure begins as well.

Lord, I want to be your disciple. At times I'm reluctant. Sometimes, I make excuses. Forgive me for missed opportunities. I offer my life, my gifts, my time, and my influence to you. Help me pay attention to the promptings of your Spirit. And use me to fish for people. In your name. Amen.

2

WALKING WITH JESUS IN THE STORMS

Right then, Jesus made the disciples get into the boat and go ahead to the other side of the lake while he dismissed the crowds. When he sent them away, he went up onto a mountain by himself to pray. Evening came and he was alone. Meanwhile, the boat, fighting a strong headwind, was being battered by the waves and was already far away from land. Very early in the morning he came to his disciples, walking on the lake. When the disciples saw him walking on the lake, they were terrified and said, "It's a ghost!" They were so frightened they screamed.

Just then Jesus spoke to them, "Be encouraged! It's me. Don't be afraid."

Peter replied, "Lord, if it's you, order me to come to you on the water."

And Jesus said, "Come."

Then Peter got out of the boat and was walking on the water toward Jesus. But when Peter saw the strong wind, he became frightened. As he began to sink, he shouted, "Lord, rescue me!"

Jesus immediately reached out and grabbed him, saying, "You man of weak faith! Why did you begin to have doubts?" When they got into the boat, the wind settled down.

Then those in the boat worshipped Jesus and said, "You must be God's Son!"

When they had crossed the lake, they landed at Gennesaret.
(Matthew 14:22-34)

LaVon and I have been going to the Lake of the Ozarks for a few weeks each summer for the last fifteen years. Our place is on the Coffman Bend of the winding ninety-four-mile-long lake, nestled among tall oak trees. It is there I go to write—in fact, I'm sitting on my porch, computer on my lap, writing this chapter.

Recently, just after sunset, a strong storm swept through our cove. White caps spread across the waves. Winds gusted above forty miles an hour. Then came the lightning and the thunder and the pouring rain. It is beautiful to watch a storm like this from my screened porch and terrifying to be on the lake in a boat when it occurs.

As the wind blew, I decided I'd better run down to the dock to make sure everything was secure, worried that the wind might sweep LaVon's kayak or paddleboard into the lake. When I got there, I was surprised to see three fishermen sitting on the dock, their small fishing boat pulled into our slip, taking shelter from the storm.

They told me they'd spent the day fishing and stopping at each bar they encountered along the lake for a drink. One of the guys had just turned forty, and this fishing trip with his buddies was a gift from his wife.

As the storm raged, I wondered, "What are the chances, with the thousands of homes that line the shore of the Lake of the Ozarks, that these fishermen would end up back in my cove and on my dock in the middle of the storm, just as I am writing a chapter of this book on Simon Peter and his fishing friends in the midst of a storm on the Sea of Galilee?"

I invited the guys to come inside our home, but they wanted to stay on the dock. So I offered them something to drink and sat down with them until the storm passed. They asked me what kind of work I did. I told them I was a pastor—a fisher of people. Instantly they wanted to talk, peppering me with questions, telling me about their lives and their boat. For the next hour we talked about God, the Bible, and life. After the storm passed, we said our good-byes. As I walked back to the house, my thoughts turned back to the story of that other storm on a lake, when Simon and his friends were facing the wind and waves, in the dark, on the Sea of Galilee.

Jesus' Boat

It's no surprise to me that when Jesus chose his home for the three years of his public ministry, he chose a fishing village on the shore of the Sea of Galilee. So many of the Gospel stories take place there. For most people who visit the Holy Land, traveling across the Sea of Galilee by boat ranks among their favorite experiences. And staying on the sea and watching the sun rise or set over the sea provides one of the most beautiful and memorable experiences of such a trip.

I mentioned in the last chapter that the Sea of Galilee, which was also called Lake Kinneret and even the Sea of Tiberias in biblical times, was thirteen miles from north to south and eight miles at its widest point, east to west. It has a surface area of forty-one thousand acres (compared to the fifty-four thousand acres of the Lake of the Ozarks) and is 141 feet deep (compared with 130 feet at its deepest at the Lake of the Ozarks). In biblical times, no one knew precisely how deep the Sea of Galilee was— it was deeper than any ropes that had been let down to measure (a process called soundings, where rope, with lead weights attached, was dropped into the a body of water to determine its depth). Hence some believed that depth of the Sea of Galilee was "unfathomable"—that is, endlessly deep, opening into the underworld.

We read again and again in the Gospels about Jesus and his disciples taking a boat across the lake. It was often the fastest way to get from point A to point B, but I suspect Jesus also just liked being on the water. There's something about traveling across the Sea of Galilee in a boat that is calming and renewing to the soul.

A common boat on the Lake of the Ozarks is about twenty-five feet from stem to stern. Today, a boat of this size is typically rated to accommodate about thirteen people. This is, we believe, almost exactly the size of the boats most frequently used on the Sea of Galilee in biblical times. Josephus, the first-century Jewish historian, tells us that there were at least 230 boats used on the Sea of Galilee.

In 1986, one of these ancient boats was found. There was a drought that year, and water levels were very low. Brothers Moshe and Yuval Lufan, fishermen and amateur archaeologists, were exploring the exposed lake bed on the northwest shore of the Sea of Galilee when they saw what looked like portions of the frame of a boat protruding from the mud. The find was excavated and discovered to be a small boat. Radiocarbon dating suggested the boat was from about 40 BC, give or take eighty

The remains of a fishing boat from the first century AD, found at the Sea of Galilee.

years. Archaeologists dated it to between 50 BC and AD 50 by examining pottery found near the boat. The boat was quickly labeled, "the Jesus boat." This boat was 27 feet long and 7.5 feet wide, and it could hold thirteen people. The boat can be seen in a museum along the lakeshore at Kibbutz Ginosar. It was designed to operate with a single mast sail or by the work of four oarsmen.

Simon had spent nearly his entire life on the shore of the Sea of Galilee and had logged thousands of hours in boats like this one, fishing and simply sailing across the lake. But on the occasion of our story, Simon would have an experience unlike any he'd ever had before.

A Storm on the Sea

Matthew, Mark, and John all tell the story of the storm at sea, though with some variations. But it is only Matthew's account that includes Peter walking on the water. The story occurs after the feeding of the multitudes (Matthew 14:13-21). Following the meal, Matthew tells us,

> *Jesus made the disciples get into the boat and go ahead to the other side of the lake while he dismissed the crowds. When he sent them away, he went up onto a mountain by himself to pray. Evening came and he was alone. Meanwhile, the boat, fighting a strong headwind, was being battered by the waves and was already far away from land.*
>
> *(Matthew 14:22-24)*

The journey should have only taken the disciples a couple of hours, were it not for the storm that came up, likely blowing them south and east. But with the storm, the little boat was being buffeted by the wind and waves, moving them a very long way from their destination, and it was all happening at night.

I've been out in the lake on many occasions when a storm blows in. It happened just last week. But you know that storms on the water must be taken seriously. Today, most boats have the convenience of a motor to get us home and off the lake quickly in the event of a storm. But the disciples had only four oars, since the sail was likely brought down to protect the mast.

So the disciples were rightly anxious as their little boat was caught in the storm. As I was writing this chapter, a terrible accident happened in a storm at Table Rock Lake, another lake in Missouri. A "duck boat"—an amphibious boat used to give tours of the lake—sank in the midst of a storm, killing seventeen people on board. There had undoubtedly been deaths on the Sea of Galilee that led the disciples to grave concern on that dark night.

I love what happens next in our story. Jesus, from the land, knew the disciples were struggling. They were too far from shore for him to literally see them struggling. But in his mind's

46

eye he could see them, and he knew they needed help. Matthew continues in his telling of the story,

> *Very early in the morning he came to his disciples, walking on the lake. When the disciples saw him walking on the lake, they were terrified and said, "It's a ghost!" They were so frightened they screamed.*
>
> *Just then Jesus spoke to them, "Be encouraged! It's me. Don't be afraid."*
>
> (Matthew 14:25-27)

Why were they terrified when they saw Jesus walking on the water? They assumed he was a spirit or a ghost. As I mentioned earlier, there was a tradition that, at the bottom of the Sea of Galilee, was a portal to the underworld, the realm of the dead. The disciples were already scared, but now they were terrified as it appeared a spirit had escaped from the underworld. Perhaps the spirit had come to take them to the realm of the dead.

Just then Jesus spoke up. I love his words, "Be encouraged! It's me! Don't be afraid."

As we'll see in a moment, hidden in this story and in Jesus' response to Peter is a clue as to the true identity of this rabbi the disciples had begun to follow. But it is important to note that the Gospel writers also wanted their readers to see Jesus coming to his disciples in their hour of need. He was watching over them even when they could not see him. This is intended to be a picture of what Jesus still does in the lives of believers when we're sailing through our own storms in the darkness.

We're meant to recognize in these stories a metaphor for what happens in our own lives. We experience tempestuous storms in life, and they can terrify us if we allow ourselves to face them alone.

Every week during worship, people at Church of the Resurrection turn in prayer request cards. We receive well over one hundred of them in a typical week. One might be from a woman whose daughter is struggling with depression. Another might be from someone whose spouse just left them. Yet another might involve someone who is fighting an addiction to drugs, alcohol, or pornography. Some are from people who recently lost their jobs. Others come from those who lost loved ones. All of these people are in the midst of storms in their lives. Some have been tossed about by the waves for months and are holding on with white knuckles for dear life. For others, the storm just blew in last week. For most, it's a frightening experience.

When we're walking through the storms that inevitably we will face, we should remember these stories of Jesus coming to the disciples on the sea. We can remember his words to them: "Be encouraged! It's me. Don't be afraid." Those three little words—don't be afraid—are the most frequently spoken words from God to human beings in Scripture. You'll find that phrase more than 140 times in your Bible.

During the storms in our lives, when the waves are crashing up against our boat and we fear we won't survive, Jesus still walks on the water to wherever we are. He gets in the boat with us. Jesus may not make the storm go away, as he did for Peter and the disciples. The cancer may still be there. The spouse may still be gone. But Jesus is riding it out with us, and somehow that makes the storm less terrifying. That is part of what the Christian's spiritual life is about. Feeling Jesus' presence with us enables us to be calmed, even if the storm is raging all around us.

Bill Brunson is a United Methodist pastor in Alabama. Some years ago, he and I were part of a group trip to the Holy Land. While we were at the Sea of Galilee, he shared his story with me. Bill and his wife married right out of college. The couple had been married for two years, with a six-month-old daughter, when Bill's wife was diagnosed with leukemia. He was in seminary and serving two little churches part-time. Throughout that spring and fall, his wife was in and out of the hospital multiple times. It gradually became clear that she was not going to get better.

She passed away just before Easter the year Bill graduated from seminary. This is what he told me about his experience:

> Throughout all of that—when the waves would be the highest and fear and anger and so much more would crash against me and even over me—I would always be reminded that I was not alone. More times than I can count, I would find myself thinking, "I just can't do this." I felt like I was in a boat on the lake and I was going to drown. And then I would suddenly feel (not hear): "We can do this together." And I would take the next step and move forward into the next day. I wish the storm had never come, but I have no doubt that Jesus' presence in my boat calmed the wind and the waves and never let me drown.

I think this is what the Gospel writers hoped their readers would understand when they included the story of Jesus walking on the water, not only that he once did what only God can do but also that he continues to come to us in the storms of life, climbs into our boat, and rides out the storm with us.

Lord, Command Me to Come to You

As we return to Matthew's telling of the story, we find the disciples uncertain if they could believe their eyes and their ears. Could that really be Jesus, walking on the turbulent water in the storm? Only Simon Peter was bold enough to speak up, and even he seemed a bit unsure. "Lord," he said, "if it's you, order me to come to you on the water" (Matthew 14:28).

Have you ever thought about what an odd thing that is to say in this situation? It sounds almost idiotic. I try to put myself in Peter's position. I don't know what Jesus is doing, or how he's doing it, but if I see him walking on the water in a storm that might cause me to drown, I imagine I would say, "Jesus, come get in the boat!" I'd even throw him a life jacket. I'd reach out my hand to help pull him in. But Peter does the opposite. He has

49

the audacity to ask Jesus to bid him to step out of the boat and walk on the water. That gives you a clue as to why Peter is the prince of the apostles. When everyone else was too scared or too confused to respond, Peter took the lead. He alone thought to himself, *"If Jesus can walk on the water, maybe I can do it too."*

Please notice an important detail here. Peter didn't just call to Jesus and step out of the boat. He waited for Jesus to bid him to step out of the boat and come to him. He did not trust in his own ability to walk on the water. But he trusted that if Jesus called him to do it, he could.

Jesus said, "Come!" And Peter stepped out of the boat. Can you imagine that? Peter had been working on the water for his entire adult life. His experience had taught him that getting out of a boat on the lake meant that a person either would have to sink or swim; walking was not an option. And in a storm like that, and being far from shore, swimming wasn't much of an option either. Yet here was Simon Peter, stepping out of the boat, no life jacket, no life buoy. Just Jesus.

Some years ago, my friend John Ortberg wrote a terrific book (he's written many terrific books) called *If You Want to Walk on Water, You've Got to Get Out of the Boat.* The book is built around this one Scripture passage. For Ortberg, the fishing boat is a metaphor that represents safety, security, the status quo, and our comfort zone. Along with discussing Peter's bold step in faith, Ortberg turns the reader's attention back to the other eleven disciples. We often knock Peter because, as we'll see in a moment, he's going to take his eyes off of Jesus and begin to sink. But notice the other eleven disciples never even thought about getting out of the boat. Ortberg calls them "boat potatoes." They stayed where they were. They remained in the boat because they were afraid of what could happen if they moved beyond it.

Ortberg raises the question, What is your boat? What is the comfort zone you are too afraid to leave behind? And how does fear keep you from experiencing a richer, more fulfilling life?

Fear is ubiquitous. It is everywhere. We struggle with fear all the time, often without even realizing it. There's a biochemical reason for this. Part of our brain is always watching out for danger, pondering at the subconscious level possible dangers and threats. Our survival can depend on a certain level of healthy fear. But fear also has an amazing capacity to keep us trapped and paralyzed. It can keep us from experiencing the life God intends for us.*

Fear keeps some people in dead-end jobs and environments so miserable that they dread going to work—and yet they come back day after day because they are afraid to go into another field that would actually excite them. I've known people who stayed in abusive marriages because they were more afraid of venturing into the unknown than of staying with their abuser.

In my office, my assistant has a couple of buttons—a "yes" button and a "no" button. They're helpful for a good laugh once in a while. When you think about it, we face situations in our lives every day that call us to say yes or say no. When fear becomes the driving force in our life, our brain reflexively pushes the "no" button. It becomes a routine. And so we say no to things to which we should say yes. We say no to a promising new opportunity— or to an invitation from Jesus to venture out in a new way that may be unfamiliar to us. We think of a thousand excuses, all of them perfectly reasonable. But when we are motivated primarily by faith rather than fear, we recognize, as Peter did, that the adventure is *outside the boat.*

Peter had come to trust Jesus just enough, even though he was scared, to say yes to Jesus' call for him to walk on a stormy sea. It is faith, and a sense of God's call, that leads us to press the "yes" button when we feel like saying no. Walking out in faith doesn't mean we know in advance how everything will work out. It means we come to trust enough to push the "yes" button in spite of our fears.

---

* If you want to read more, see my book *Unafraid: Living with Courage and Hope in Uncertain Times* (New York: Convergent, 2018).

Which kind of Christian are you? Are you the kind who is more likely to press the "no" button? If so, you're in pretty good company. Eleven of the twelve disciples in the boat that night pressed the "no" button, too. It didn't mean they were no longer followers of Jesus. But the one who said "yes" experienced, at least for a moment, the kind of amazing faith walk that Jesus wants for all of us.

What does it look like to say yes when we feel like saying no? I can think of so many examples just from my own congregation, and I imagine you can do the same. Many of them are just simple illustrations; walking in faith doesn't always involve something as dramatic as leaving everything else behind to follow Jesus into the unknown.

The last time I preached on this story was also the day before our quarterly blood drive at the church. I noted that there were likely many in our congregation who had never given blood; their anxiety or fear, whether of a needle or the sight of blood, had kept them from doing something that could save the life of someone else. I invited them to step out of the boat.

The next day, as I gave blood, I had a dozen people come to me to say that they were "stepping out of the boat," including one woman who told me that she was sixty years old and had always been afraid to give blood. When I spoke about the blood drive in the context of this story, she said she felt Jesus calling her out of the boat, to lay aside her fears, and to join him on the water. After all, she noted, he gave his blood for us. I felt I could do the same. And she did it! She gave the "gift of life" and survived, and she felt joy knowing she had helped to save someone else's life.

I think about the people in our congregation who go to serve in the inner city or travel from Kansas City to serve in other parts of the world. We recognize that this entails stepping outside of our comfort zones, which is another way of saying, "getting out of the boat." Here's what I find: virtually always these persons return from serving feeling joyful.

Rescue Me

Let's go back to the story. After Peter stepped out of the boat, he actually walked on water! But then, as Matthew tells us, Peter noticed the strong wind, and it frightened him. When he became frightened, he began to sink. He cried out, "Lord, rescue me!" And Jesus immediately reached out his hand and lifted Peter up.

When I read that line, "Jesus immediately reached out and grabbed him," I think of Thomas Dorsey, the father of black gospel. Dorsey wrote the hymn, "Precious Lord, Take My Hand," after his wife, Nettie, died in childbirth. Part of the lyric in the first verse takes us back to this story: "Through the storm, through the night / Lead me on to the light." When he wrote this hymn, Thomas Dorsey was sinking, and the only one who might rescue him from his inconsolable grief was the one who took Simon Peter's hand. Sometimes, that's our only prayer, too, when the storms of life are raging around us: "Save me, Lord. Rescue me. Help!"

After rescuing him, Jesus said to Peter, "You man of weak faith! Why did you begin to have doubts?" The Gospel doesn't tell us anything about Jesus' tone of voice or inflection. But I don't think he was really chastising Peter. After all, Peter showed more faith than the eleven who remained in the boat. I think Jesus was expressing the kind of disappointment I would express to my daughters as they were growing up and gave up too quickly on something they could have conquered if only they'd kept at it. I imagine Jesus meaning something like: "Peter, why did you look away? I had you. You didn't need to worry! If you had only trusted me."

As it so often is with Peter, just after we see him take two remarkable steps forward in faith, we see him take one step back. This is the picture we'll see again and again of Simon— faithful and bold, yet easily confused, deterred, and oh so flawed. Maybe that's why we love him so much. He reminds us of ourselves. He reminds us that, despite our flaws, we can still be followers of Jesus. He will still rescue, befriend, and use us.

Who Is This Man?

Matthew tells us that "When they got into the boat, the wind settled down. Then those in the boat worshipped Jesus and said, "You must be God's Son!" (Matthew 14:32-33).

The Greek word for worship, *proskuneo,* implies giving honor and great respect. Literally it means to lean toward or bow before someone to kiss them, usually on their hand or their feet. It is a term describing the honor most often reserved for God. But it could be used in the context of paying homage to someone who had just done something amazing (like rescuing twelve guys who were going to drown at sea!).

Yet there is something more going on here. This astounding miracle was revealing something profound about the man standing in the boat with them. In some sense, they had experienced in that moment an encounter with God.

What kind of man walks on water? What kind of man calms the storms? Sailors and fishermen knew certain scriptures well—scriptures that related to the waters. Psalm 77:19 notes,

> *Your way was through the sea,*
> > *your path, through the mighty waters;*
> > *yet your footprints were unseen. (NRSV)*

Job would describe God as one who, "trampled the waves of the Sea" (Job 9:8 NRSV). Throughout the Hebrew Bible, it is God alone who controls the wind and the waves. Simon's father was named after a prophet who came to understand this only too well. Every sailor and fisherman who made his living on the Sea of Galilee knew the words of Psalm 89:8-9 (NIV):

Who is like you, LORD God Almighty?...

You rule over the surging sea;
when its waves mount up, you still them.

And Psalm 107, thought to be the psalm of the sailors, reads:

Some of the redeemed had gone out on the ocean
in ships,
making their living on the high seas...
The waves went as high as the sky;
they crashed down to the depths.
The sailors' courage melted at this terrible situation...
So they cried out to the LORD in their distress,
and God brought them out safe from their
desperate circumstances.
God quieted the storm to a whisper;
the sea's waves were hushed. (23-29)

Who is it that calms the winds and the waves? Who delivers the sailors from harm? The Jewish fishermen would have known the answer to that question: It is God.

The disciples acknowledged in the darkness as they knelt before Jesus on the boat, "You must be God's Son!" (Matthew 14:33). This was the first time in the Gospels that the disciples declared Jesus to be God's Son, the first time they declared this kind of faith in him. They had known him as a carpenter from Nazareth. They knew him as a rabbi who called them to be fishers of people. They had seen him perform some miracles. Though the disciples didn't yet understand the affirmations the church would one day make about him—that Jesus was "fully God" and "fully human," that he was God the Son in human flesh—they had nevertheless experienced God's presence in this man that night on the sea.

There's another clue as to the identity of this man. When Jesus first spoke to the disciples as he came walking to them on water, he said, "Be encouraged" and "Don't be afraid." But he also said, "It's me!" In the original Greek, the phrase is *ego eimi*, which literally translates as "I am." When you read it literally, at first blush that seems like an unusual thing to say. "Be encouraged and don't be afraid because I am." What exactly does that mean?

To understand what Jesus was telling the disciples, we have to go all the way back to Moses. You may remember that when Moses first encountered God, who got his attention with a burning bush, God said he wanted Moses to go back to Egypt and deliver the children of Israel from slavery. And you may recall that, during this dialogue, Moses asked God, "When the people ask which god has sent me, what should I tell them? What is your name?"

God's reply to Moses' question was, "I Am Who I Am. So say to the Israelites, 'I Am has sent me to you'" (Exodus 3:14). In Hebrew, the word for I Am is YHWH or Yahweh (or as we sometimes render it, Jehovah). We often see Jesus using these words, *ego eimi* in John's Gospel, but here in Matthew's telling of our story, Jesus speaks these same words. When he does, he's giving a nod to the divine name for God in the Hebrew Bible, as well as a clue to his identity.

Coming to Us on the Water

As I was writing this book, a terrible accident took place on the Lake of the Ozarks, just a few miles from our place there. Five young adults were on a boat ride late at night. The moon had set. There was cloud cover. Somehow, the driver of the boat had not seen the rock bluff in front of them. Three young people were killed, and two were injured. The next day, I learned that one of the girls who had been injured and one who had died were connected to our church.

As I prepared the funeral message for Hailey, I was drawn to the Scripture we've been focusing on in this story. I shared with those present that I didn't believe Jesus willed this accident. I don't think he causes boating accidents or takes children away from their parents. God does not typically circumvent the laws of physics to keep accidents from happening. So, what does God do in the midst of the tragedies that occur in life, the storms that come our way?

I told those at Hailey's service the story we've been focusing on of Jesus coming to Peter and the disciples on the water. Then I shared with them this reflection:

> That story was told and retold by the early church because it painted a picture of what Jesus does in our lives. He still comes to us on the water, in the darkness, in the storms of life, in the tragedy and pain—he still walks on the water, steps into our boats, or dives into the water with us. He holds us and says to us, "It is me, do not be afraid."

> In the middle of the night, about the 47-mile marker on the Lake of the Ozarks, I believe Jesus was there with Hailey and each of the others. I think he was whispering to them, "I have got a hold of you. It's me. Don't be afraid." He didn't wish for this accident. He didn't plan it, or cause it, or will it. But when it did happen, he held Hailey near and said, "You are mine, you are safe in my arms."

In the Arms of Our Master

Late one night, as I sat on our back porch at our home in Kansas City, perhaps around the time of night that the disciples found themselves in such distress on the Sea of Galilee—there was a terrific thunderstorm raging outside. I was preparing a sermon on this story of Jesus coming to the disciples in the storm. Our porch has vinyl windows that we can close to keep the rain out, so I remained outside, secure from the rain, but enjoying the thunder claps as I prepared the message.

I was fine, but our little dog Maybelle is scared of storms. Amid all the thunder crashing and lightning flashing, she came out on the porch, and she was shaking all over with fear. Some time ago, LaVon bought a "thunder shirt" for Maybelle. You wrap it around her tightly and attach it with Velcro, and it's supposed to calm her down when there's a storm. So I found Maybelle's thunder shirt and put it on her, and then I went back to my sermon. A few minutes later, she returned to the porch, and she was still shaking as much as she had been earlier. The storm was so bad that even the thunder shirt didn't help.

So I picked Maybelle up and placed her next to me on the sofa where I was working. She laid her chin on my knee, in front of my laptop, and I put my arm on top of her as an armrest while I continued to type. Pretty soon, I could feel that Maybelle no longer was quivering. Then I looked down and noticed that she had fallen fast asleep. The thunder and lightning continued outside, just as bad as they had been before. What had changed was that Maybelle was by her master's side. Somehow, she knew that if her master was there, everything was going to be okay. I think that's part of what we're meant to learn from this story.

We are called to remember that in the midst of life's worst storms when we're scared and don't know how we are going to make it through, our Master still comes to us, walking on the water, through the storm. He comes to us, steps in the boat with us, calming the wind and the waves.

Lord, help me be the disciple you want me to be. Help me answer your call to be brave and to climb out of the boat, to leave my comfort zone, to walk with you. When I am beset by storms and sinking, take my hand and rescue me. Climb into my boat and calm the wind and the waves. In your holy name. Amen.

3

BEDROCK OR STUMBLING BLOCK?

Now when Jesus came to the area of Caesarea Philippi, he asked his disciples, "Who do people say the ~~Human One~~ is?" Son of Man

They replied, "Some say John the Baptist, others Elijah, and still others Jeremiah or one of the other prophets."

He said, "And what about you? Who do you say that I am?"

Simon Peter said, "You are the Christ, the Son of the living God." Messiah

Then Jesus replied, "Happy are you, Simon son of Jonah, because no human has shown this to you. Rather my Father who is in heaven has shown

v.18 the gates of Hades
NIV will not overcome it

you. I tell you that you are Peter. And I'll build my
church on this rock. The gates of the underworld
won't be able to stand against it. I'll give you
the keys of the kingdom of heaven. Anything
you fasten on earth will be fastened in heaven.
Anything you loosen on earth will be loosened in
heaven."…

Bind

From that time Jesus began to show his disciples
that he had to go to Jerusalem and suffer many
things from the elders, chief priests, and legal
experts, and that he had to be killed and raised on
the third day. Then Peter took hold of Jesus and,
scolding him, began to correct him: "God forbid,
Lord! This won't happen to you." But he turned to
Peter and said, "Get behind me, Satan. You are a
stone that could make me stumble, for you are not
thinking God's thoughts but human thoughts."
(Matthew 16:13-19, 21-23)

All three of the Synoptic Gospels—Matthew, Mark, and Luke—tell the story of Peter's dramatic declaration of faith, when he boldly proclaimed that Jesus was the long-awaited Messiah. Matthew and Mark tell us where it happened: "in the area of Caesarea Philippi." The authors' inclusion of this detail may indicate that the location for this story was important.

Caesarea Philippi was in a predominantly non-Jewish area long associated with the worship of pagan deities.* Located about twenty-five miles north of the Sea of Galilee, at the base of Mount Hermon, it takes about an hour by car to drive there along the winding roads passing through the easternmost part of the Golan Heights. It would have taken the apostles a couple of days on foot to make this journey north. This was a remote and out of the way place for them. One might imagine that when Jesus told

---

* Going all the way back to Judges where the people of the tribe of Dan set up idols to worship in the north. See Judges 18.

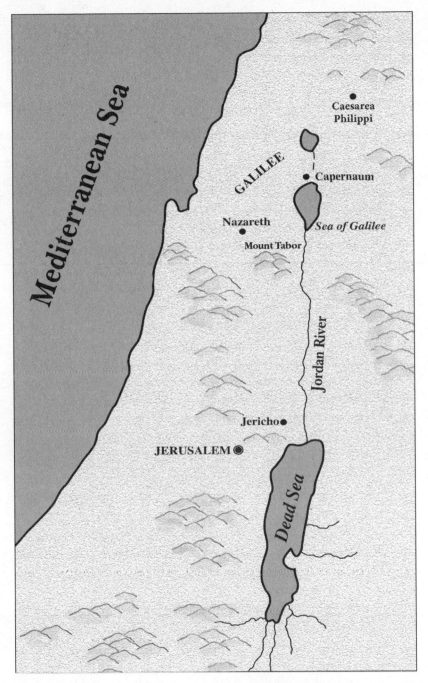

the disciples they were heading north, to Caesarea, they might have asked, "Why on earth would we travel up there?" To the disciples, as to the readers of the Gospels who are familiar with first-century geography, it was an odd trip to take.

For centuries, Caesarea Philippi was not a city, but a place of pagan worship known as Panias (or Paneas). Pan, the Greek god of nature, flocks, and the wild, with the torso of a man and hind quarters of a goat, was worshiped at places of great natural beauty (the ancients, like us, were moved to wonder and worship by nature's beauty—consider the words to "How Great Thou Art"). The area then known as Caesarea Philippi is as beautiful a place as you can find in this part of the world. Today, the place is called the Hermon Stream Nature Reserve, or more commonly, Banias.

As ancient visitors came to this place, they would pass a waterfall, which was the largest most people in that region had ever seen at thirty feet tall. Just a few paces farther, a river was found to be flowing out of the base of Mount Hermon. Today that river is called Hermon Stream. It, like the waterfall whose water joins it, is fed by the snowmelt from Mount Hermon and serves as one of the headwaters of the Jordan River. A seventy-foot-tall sheer rock wall arises from the trees, broken only by a large cave. In ancient times, at the back of this cave, a chasm opened up, at the bottom of which flowed the underground spring that spilled out of the mount below. Those worshiping Pan would come bringing their sacrifices, sheep, and other offerings, and drop them into the chasm. Attempts had been made to determine how deep the water was, but no amount of rope with lead weights tied to the end was sufficient to reach the bottom. It was thought by some to be a chasm to the underworld—to Hades, the realm of the dead.

By the time Jesus brought his disciples here, a temple had been built in front of the cave, and others beside it, the foundations of which can still be seen. One of these temples is believed to be the one built by King Herod the Great in 20 BC

Hermon Stream flows out of the base of Mount Hermon, near where Jesus asked the disciples "Who do you say that I am?"

and dedicated to Augustus Caesar. Josephus, the first-century Jewish historian, describes the reason for its construction in his *War of the Jews* with these words, "And when Caesar had further bestowed upon him [Herod] another additional country, he built there also a temple of white marble, hard by the fountains of Jordan: the place is called Panium" (*Wars* 1:21:3).

After King Herod's death, his son Philip built a city adjacent to the shrines, making it his administrative center in the north and calling it Caesarea in honor of the emperor. Since his father had built another city by that name on the Mediterranean, this Caesarea became known as Philip's Caesarea, or Caesarea Philippi.

The site is as beautiful today as it was in ancient times before the city was built. Few Christians who visit the Holy Land come to this site—it simply takes up too much time to really enjoy the place. To hike the nature trails and explore the archaeological site, counting the driving time there and back, it is the better part of a day. But when you visit, it begins to make sense why Jesus brought his disciples here to ask them a crucial question: "Who do you say that I am?"

Who Do You Say That I Am?

I picture Jesus sitting with his disciples in the shadow of the shrines to Pan and the emperor when he asks his disciples an odd question: Who do people say that the Human One (often translated Son of Man) is? "Human One" was a cryptic term Jesus often used of himself, speaking of himself in the third person. The phrase could mean, simply, human being, and often appears in that sense, particularly in the many times the phrase is used of Ezekiel the prophet. The phrase appears as a messianic term in Daniel where the prophet describes a vision of seeing "a human one" or one like a "son of man" coming before God's throne, and this man was given "rule, glory and kingship" by God. Concerning this man Daniel said, "his kingship is indestructible" (Daniel 7:14).

When Jesus asked his disciples, "Who do the people say the Human One is?" They responded, "Some say John the Baptist, others Elijah, and still others Jeremiah or one of the other prophets." John, who had been put to death by Herod Antipas by this time, was considered a prophet. Elijah and Jeremiah were clearly prophets. So the disciples are noting that many consider the "Human One" to be a prophet. They presumed that, by "the Human One" he was referring to himself, but I'm guessing they weren't completely sure. Jesus then offers another query: "And what about you? Who do *you* say that I am?" (Matthew 16:13-15).

Have you ever been somewhere, in a classroom, at the office, or among friends, where someone asks a question, and you are pretty sure you know the answer, but you are not 100 percent sure, and you don't want to look foolish or stupid, so you remain quiet? I have. And that's how I picture what happened there by the Hermon Stream, in the shadow of the temples to Pan and Caesar, with the sheer exposed rock face of Mount Hermon above the disciples. I can see them looking down in silence, not willing to risk giving the wrong answer and not wanting to demonstrate that they are not entirely sure.

Up to this point, Jesus had not identified himself as the Messiah. The disciples had watched him heal the sick, cast out demons, feed the multitudes, calm the wind and the waves of the sea, even walk on water. But he had never come right out and said he was the Messiah. And they had never come right out and asked. But Jesus brought them here, to this place, to ask them this question. And who was the only disciple courageous, brash, or foolish enough to offer an answer? Simon Peter.

You Are the Messiah

Matthew records Peter's answer as one of the great declarations of faith in any of the Gospels: "You are the Christ, the Son of the living God." This is an important answer, though it doesn't represent everything Christians eventually came to believe about Jesus in light of his death and resurrection. If you were asked, "Who do you say that Jesus is?" you would likely add a host of other titles and descriptors. He is the Savior. He is the risen Lord. With John's Gospel you might call him "the Word made flesh," or with the Nicene Creed, "God from God, Light from Light, true God from true God." Peter did not use these words on that day. He did, however, boldly claim that Jesus was "the Christ, the Son of the living God."

Let's unpack this a bit, because at the very least we need to understand what Peter was declaring. Christ, of course, is not Jesus' last name. The New Testament was written in Greek, and *Christos* is the Greek equivalent of the Hebrew word from which we have our word *Messiah*. It literally means "anointed one." In the Hebrew Bible, the Old Testament, priests and kings were anointed with oil, as were the sacred objects in the Tabernacle and temple. The act of anointing something was a way of setting it apart for God's purposes. As it related to priests and kings, it was a sign that the individual had been chosen by God and set apart to rule or lead as God's instrument and servant. While there were many kings and priests who were anointed to rule and lead the people, the prophets spoke of an ideal king, one who would rule with righteousness and justice as God's servant.

This hope for the ideal king, the coming king, not just an anointed one but _the_ Anointed One, became particularly pronounced when the land of Israel was ruled by foreign powers, when the people were oppressed, or when the national leaders were turning away from God. Faithful Jews would search the Scriptures for any hint or promise concerning the king that was to come, who would usher in God's kingdom on earth. Christ or Messiah was a title that meant the King the Jewish people had been waiting for. This is what Peter meant when he answered Jesus' question, "Who do you say that I am?" As the others sat in silence, Simon spoke up and said, "You are the Christ."

The Jewish people in the first century had come to believe the Messiah would be a human being with extraordinary leadership gifts. He would be courageous and bold. He would grow up devoted to God and to God's justice and righteousness. But he would also be a great warrior. Part of the reason Jews continued to remember the story of the Maccabees and name their children after them was because the Maccabee brothers and their father had painted a picture of the kind of Messiah they believed God would send again. They awaited a warrior-priest-king who would raise an army to cast out the Romans, call the Jewish people to repentance, purify themselves before God, and then serve as a light to the nations. To borrow a phrase from our own day, most Jews of the time of Jesus anticipated a Messiah who would "make Israel great again."

This is likely what Simon and the other disciples anticipated in the coming Christ, which is why the others may have remained quiet. Jesus met some of the expectations—calling people to repentance, teaching people about the kingdom of God, bringing healing and deliverance from those who were afflicted. But he showed no signs of raising up an army of rebels. In fact, he had taught his followers to love their enemies, to turn the other cheek when struck, and to do what the Romans commanded.

It is easy to understand the hesitation in responding to Jesus' question.

You Are the Son of God

Simon didn't simply say that Jesus was the Christ. He also called him, "the Son of the Living God." That's a very important statement, too, and it deserves some unpacking of its own.

"Son of God" was a royal title. In Psalm 2:7 the psalmist, presumably David, is acknowledged as God's son. We find the same thing in 2 Samuel 7:14 where God says of Solomon, "I will be a father to him, and he will be a son to me." The Messiah would be a "son of David"—that is, a descendant of David—but he would also be a son of God. In fact, both of these two passages, Psalm 2:7 and 2 Samuel 7:14, were seen by many in Jesus' day as foreshadowing the coming of the Messiah. They did not necessarily understand this as David, Solomon, or the Messiah being in some sense divine. Rather, they understood it to mean David, Solomon, and the Messiah having with God a relationship of son to Father.

Yet, as we saw in the last chapter, Simon has twice knelt before Jesus, both times in a boat, as he saw Jesus do what no ordinary human should have the power to do. Did Simon have a clear "Christology" worked out at this point? No. But he had experienced the power of God through Jesus. At the very least, when Simon spoke up saying, "You are the Christ, the Son of the Living God," he meant that Jesus was the anticipated king sent by God, with whom God had a special relationship, as a Father to a son. But it seems likely that Simon was beginning to grasp that there might be something more to Jesus than met the eye.

Which takes us back to the unusual place Jesus brought his disciples for this conversation. He brought them to a city, Caesarea, named in honor of the emperor, and in the shadow of the white marble temple dedicated to Augustus. Augustus, during his lifetime and years after his death, was hailed as

Savior, Lord, and High Priest. But most often in his lifetime, he was known as Emperor Caesar, son of a god. He was the son of a god—in Latin, *divi filius*. He was the son of a god because his adopted father, Julius Caesar, who hinted at his own divine status during his lifetime was formally declared divine by the Roman Senate at his death. At Augustus's death, he, too, was deified by the senate. Standing in this place, Jesus asks his disciples, Who do you say that I am? And Peter replies, "You are the Christ [God's anointed ruler], the Son of the *living* God."

Peter's response to Jesus' question was something of a rebuke to the claims of the emperor. Jesus, he was declaring, wasn't merely *a* son of a dead god, as Augustus Caesar was. He was *the* Son of the living God.

Christians continue to join Simon Peter in this statement of faith. I wake up every morning and yield my life to Jesus, hailing him as my Christ, my King. What I know about God is largely due to what I've seen, heard, and learned about Jesus. He is, in Paul's words, "the image of the invisible God" (Colossians 1:15), or as the Gospel of John describes him, he is God's word wrapped in human flesh. In John, Jesus says it this way, "If you've seen me, you've seen the Father." (See John 14:9.) Augustus may have been a reflection of his great uncle and adopted father, Julius Caesar. Jesus, Christians believe, was a reflection of his heavenly Father, the Creator of heaven and earth.

You Are the Rock

Upon hearing Simon's response, Jesus affirmed it with the enthusiasm of a teacher when one of her or his pupils finally speaks up with the right answer, "Yes! Well done, you've got it!"

But he went much further than that. You'll remember that John's Gospel records Jesus giving Simon a nickname at their first meeting. He had called him, in Aramaic, *Kephas* (Cephas), and in Greek, *Petros*—both of which mean "Rock." It is here, in Matthew's Gospel, that we find Jesus giving Simon this remarkable name.

"Happy are you, Simon son of Jonah, because no human has shown this to you. Rather my Father who is in heaven has shown you. I tell you that you are Peter. And I'll build my church on this rock. The gates of the underworld won't be able to stand against it."

(Matthew 16:17-18)

There before this massive wall of stone, the base of Mount Hermon, Jesus once more tells Simon he sees something in him that, quite possibly, no one else saw or could see, likely not even Simon himself. It was his willingness to take risks, his boldness and courage, his conviction and commitment, that would made him a rock upon which Jesus would build his community.

Once more, you can't miss the important connection between the place where Jesus spoke to the disciples and what he said there. "I tell you that you are Peter," Jesus says to Peter. "You are *Rock*." Jesus goes on, "and on this rock I will build my new community—my church." The Greek word for rock Jesus uses here, *petra,* doesn't typically just mean a stone; the Greek word for that is *lithos* (from which we have the word lithograph) No, *petra* typically signifies a rock ledge, a cliff, a massive rock. And Jesus called Simon, in Greek, *Petros*, against the backdrop of the seventy-foot-tall wall of rock rising behind them, the petra upon which Mount Hermon stood. Once again, being in the place these words were spoken impacts how you hear them. Simon Peter wouldn't just be a rock or a stone. He would be a massive rock, the foundation, upon which Jesus would establish his church.

Though Jesus seldom calls Simon by his new name, Peter, the early church nearly always used this name. After the birth of the early church, when Simon Peter's preaching and teaching, his witness and his ministry, even his imprisonment, played such a key role in the development of the Christian community, he was nearly always known as Rock.

In a sense, we're all laying a foundation upon which the lives and faith of others is being built. If you are a parent or grandparent, you are laying a foundation for your children and grandchildren's lives. If you are a schoolteacher, you are doing the same for your students. If you are in leadership in business or in politics or in some other arena of life, you are laying a foundation for those you are influencing, those looking up to you, and those coming after you. Every time you encourage, teach, or invest in the life of someone else, you are laying a foundation. We are all *Petros* in some way or another, hopefully helping to lay a good foundation upon which others develop and grow.

Whose Church?

But Peter wasn't simply called by Jesus to influence people's lives; Jesus said he would be the rock upon which Jesus would build his church. The Greek word translated as church is *ekklesia*—it literally means "called out ones"—and was a word that could be used of any kind of gathering or community But Jesus doesn't simply say that Peter will build a community for the sake of community. The *ekklesia* Jesus intended to build upon Peter, using Peter and his faithfulness, service, and sacrifice, would be *Jesus'* church: "On this *petra* I will build *my* church," Jesus said (see Matthew 16:18 NRSV, emphasis added).

This verse marks the first time in the Gospels that we find the word *church*. But this church isn't just any assembly or community of people gathered together; it is Christ's people, his community. The church belongs to Jesus.

The church is also not a building, but a people belonging to the Lord. The English word *church* comes from the German word *kirche*, which is related to the Greek word *kuriakon* that means "belonging to the Lord." So the church is Christ's church, not ours. Notice, too, that Jesus is the one who will build it, "On this rock *I will build* my church," he says (Matthew 16:18 NRSV, emphasis added).

The central campus of the church I serve recently completed construction of its permanent sanctuary. There were hundreds of pages of construction documents, perhaps thousands, I don't know. There were hundreds of skilled workers involved, but every one of them ultimately took their direction from Loren Ahles, the design principal, whose architectural vision all of the other architects, engineers, and contractors were seeking to bring to life.

Ultimately, if we are to be the church Jesus seeks to build—his church—then our task is to understand his "architectural" vision for his church: What does he want the local *ekklesia* you are a part of to be and to do? Peter's confession of faith, that Jesus was the Christ, the King, the son of the living God, was the conviction upon which Christ's church would be built. But implicit in this confession of faith is the central focus of Jesus' preaching and teaching: the Kingdom of God in which God's will is done on earth as it is in heaven.

Later in our New Testament, we find the first of two letters attributed to Peter, and in describing the church, he speaks of stones. He uses the Greek word *lithoi* to describe the role Christians are meant to play in building Christ's church,

> *Come to him, a living stone, though rejected by mortals yet chosen and precious in God's sight, and like living stones, let yourselves be built into a spiritual house, to be a holy priesthood, to offer spiritual sacrifices acceptable to God through Jesus Christ.*
>
> *(1 Peter 2:4-5 NRSV)*

The church is not a physical building, but a people, who together are a spiritual house. And all of us are meant to see ourselves as living stones, the building blocks of a community and movement through which God is working to heal and transform the world.

There are many things that can derail a church. Among these is when the members forget that the church belongs to Jesus, and they begin to act like it is their church. A second, closely linked to the first, is when a church forgets its mission of continuing the ministry of Jesus in the world, and instead becomes inwardly focused. A third is when a congregation becomes unwilling to change, developing hearts of stone that are unpliable and ultimately of little use to God. Jesus seeks something different for his church—he wants us to be living rocks, together parts of the spiritual house that God is building.

The Gates of Hades

Jesus continues, "The gates of the underworld won't be able to stand against it." We usually hear this translated as, "The gates of hell shall not prevail against it" (Matthew 16:18 KJV). I misunderstood these words for many years. In my mind I transposed the meaning—I read them as if they were saying, "the gates of the church are strong enough to withstand the onslaught of hell." But that isn't at all what Jesus said to Simon Peter about the church that would be built upon Peter's conviction, witness, and service. Jesus says that the *gates of Hades* are not strong enough to withstand the *onslaught of the church*. This implies that the church is meant to be actively engaged in the world; when the church is doing what Christ calls her to do, the gates of Hades cannot long prevail.

Hades is the Greek word used here. While it is often translated as hell, Hades was actually most often seen as the realm of the dead—the underworld thought to be the place of the dead until the resurrection. Once again, the place where this story occurs is interesting. As I mentioned above, in the back of Pan's cave was a deep chasm. Within it was water, constantly moving before it flowed out of the mountain and formed the stream that flowed into the Jordan River. Centuries ago, the chasm was sealed. Like the Sea of Galilee, no one had been able to determine how deep the water was, and hence it was seen as another portal to Hades, to the underworld.

In the early church, the idea developed that while Jesus was in the tomb, he descended to the underworld, broke open the gates of Hades, and liberated those who had been captive there. This is called the "harrowing of hell." Certainly, in his resurrection Jesus dealt definitively with death. But I wonder if Jesus' words about the gates of Hades are also a way of saying that the church he hoped to build would have power to overcome death. This includes physical death, through the promise of Easter and the resurrection from the dead. But it also means the power to overcome the things that represent spiritual and emotional death, such as hopelessness, despair, addiction, oppression, poverty, and sin.

Jesus goes on to tell Peter, "I'll give you the keys of the kingdom of heaven. Anything you fasten on earth will be fastened in heaven. Anything you loosen on earth will be loosened in heaven" (Matthew 16:19). This is an important statement Jesus makes, and an important authority he is conveying to Peter, then presumably to the other leaders in the church. Binding and loosing were terms applied to the leading rabbis when they debated the law and how to interpret and apply it. What they forbade was bound; what they permitted was loosened. With this statement, Jesus was giving Peter—and, through him, the church—authority to interpret Scripture and to practice church discipline. In John 20, Jesus would use similar terms to describe the power to forgive; but here in Matthew, the authority seems most closely tied to the traditional rabbinical work of interpreting and applying Scripture.

Jesus' statement, by the way, is why in Christian art you'll often see Simon Peter portrayed with keys. Keys are a prominent part of the official flag and crest of the Vatican, too, because Roman Catholics regard Peter as the first bishop of Rome—that is, the first pope.

In Jesus' time, protective walls surrounded cities, and people entered the city through gates built into the walls. (You can still pass through some of the various gates in the old city of Jerusalem.) The gates had heavy locks that were opened with keys. Up through the Middle Ages and even beyond, many cities were small kingdoms unto themselves. So if someone gave you the "keys to the kingdom," it meant that you had the power to decide who could come in and who was left out. In essence that was what Jesus told Peter.

Jesus' words to Peter were a tremendous affirmation of Simon. It must have felt a bit like a huge promotion. Jesus not only affirmed Peter's faith; he established his authority.

A Suffering King

Now the story abruptly changes direction. Jesus told the disciples not to tell anyone that he was the Messiah. Many of the Jews and Romans assumed that the promised Messiah would be a figure like the Maccabees, who would lead an armed rebellion to drive out the Romans. Because of this assumption, publicly declaring that Jesus was the Messiah would immediately draw those seeking armed rebellion and would ensure those in political power would take note and imprison or kill Jesus.

Matthew then writes, "From that time Jesus began to show his disciples that he had to go to Jerusalem and suffer many things from the elders, chief priests, and legal experts, and that he had to be killed and raised on the third day" (Matthew 16:21). This was shocking, disconcerting, and unnerving to the disciples. They, too, were likely expecting Jesus to liberate the Jewish people from Roman rule. Based upon the multitudes who had gathered to hear him and the amazing things that he had done, they expected his leadership and popularity to grow and that he would lead a religious revival among the people. What they were not expecting was that Jesus would suffer and be put to death by the religious leadership in Jerusalem.

It is tragic that the religious leadership of Jesus' day would be the ones to insist upon his death. Jesus had challenged their interpretations of Scripture. His actions, particularly his violations of their Sabbath rules, had rubbed them the wrong way. His association with "sinners" and the broken, which won the hearts of many in the crowd, was deemed impious. His popularity had raised the religious leaders' insecurities. And his occasional critiques of the scribes and Pharisees had won him few friends among them. History is littered with the stories like these of ultra-religious people missing the point, and ultimately acting in ways that were the antithesis of God's call to love.

Religious zeal, when coupled with an absolute conviction that one is right and an amnesia regarding God's call to love, can lead religious people to do the most irreligious things.

Before his conversion, St. Paul gained notoriety for harassing, arresting, and even stoning the followers of Jesus. He believed he was doing God's work. Later the tables would be turned, and Paul himself would be harassed and ultimately put to death at the insistence of religious leaders. It was worshipers of the old Roman gods that cheered as the Christians were fed to the lions. But soon, Christian bishops were using the "keys to the Kingdom" to anathematize and excommunicate those who didn't conform to their understanding of the faith. Over the centuries it was religious leaders, or secular leaders appealing to the religiosity of their people, that led the Crusades, the Inquisition, the pogroms, the religious wars, burnings at the stake—all in the name of a crucified Messiah who called people to love their enemies.

Of course, Christians are not alone in this. Nearly every religion has its zealots ready to destroy, in the name of God, those with whom it disagrees. Atheists frequently level this as a critique against religion, but I've known atheists who were as adamant in their orthodoxy as any fundamentalist, and there have been millions slaughtered in officially atheistic regimes in the name of ideological purity.

Moving beyond religion, we see this same impulse today in the political and ideological polarization in our country. As I write this chapter, we're in the midst of another election season, and the mudslinging and character assassination that's happening in sixty-second spots on the local television stations remind me of why most good people don't want to run for office. Who wants to subject themselves to this?

Jesus knew this, and he knew what was to come if he were to faithfully preach the kingdom of God in Jerusalem. He knew he would die. He had not only reconciled himself to this fact, but he believed that his death would actually serve God's redemptive purposes—that by his death he would draw people to God.

But Peter could not see this. He did not understand. So the man who had just boldly proclaimed that Jesus was the Christ, who Jesus had just given the keys to the Kingdom, "took hold of Jesus and, scolding him, began to correct him: 'God forbid, Lord! This won't happen to you'" (Matthew 16:22).

At this point in the story, Simon Peter followed a pattern that by now should be familiar. Just after taking a great step forward in faith, he took a step back. He couldn't process the idea of a suffering Messiah. Perhaps he was so fixated on the words about Jesus' death that he couldn't hear what Jesus went on to say about his resurrection. Once more, we see both the faithful and flawed side of Peter. He correctly and boldly proclaimed that Jesus is the Christ, the Son of the Living God, but could not conceive of the kind of Messiah Jesus was, or the mission he had come to pursue.

Peter didn't just speak to Jesus in response; he "took hold" of him. Then, as Matthew tells us, he scolded Jesus and "began to correct him: 'God forbid, Lord. This won't happen to you'" (Matthew 16:22). Imagine this scene for a moment, with Simon scolding and correcting the one who walked on water and calmed the storms. Bold and foolish; faithful, yet flawed.

76

Get Behind Me, Satan

Listen to Jesus' response to Simon: "Get behind me, Satan. You are a stone that could make me stumble, for you are not thinking God's thoughts but human thoughts" (Matthew 16:23). This seems a bit harsh, and it's not hard to imagine Peter's embarrassment and hurt upon hearing Jesus' words.

Once more, Peter represents us, the everyday disciple. I suspect that there have been many times in my life where my heart was in the right place, but I was not thinking God's thoughts. Instead, I was analyzing the situation from my very human perspective. There are times we make important decisions based upon our own logic, spending little or no time praying or seeking to understand God's thoughts.

I'm reminded of Samuel, who'd been sent to anoint one of the sons of Jesse to be Israel's next king. He sees the oldest, strongest son of Jesse and assumes that God has chosen him to be Israel's next king. But just before Samuel pours the oil on the man's head God says, "Not this one! You are judging by outward appearances. I judge the heart." It was the youngest, least likely of Jesse's sons that God had chosen to be Israel's next king. In Isaiah God says it this way: "My thoughts are not your thoughts, nor are your ways my ways, says the LORD" (Isaiah 55:8 NRSV). There at Caesarea Philippi, Simon couldn't yet comprehend that the transformation of the world Jesus sought to bring would come through suffering and a cross.

But why did Jesus use such a harsh word to correct Simon? "Get behind me, Satan!" Matthew surely wants us to remember the scene at the beginning of Jesus' ministry. He had been compelled by the Spirit to spend forty days fasting and praying in the wilderness of Judea. There Satan tempted him and tested his resolve. Here's the account of the final temptation in the wilderness in Matthew's Gospel:

> *Then the devil brought him to a very high mountain and showed him all the kingdoms of the world and*

their glory. He said, "I'll give you all these if you bow down and worship me."

Jesus responded, "Go away, Satan, because it's written, You will worship the Lord your God and serve only him.*"

(Matthew 4:8-10)

What was the devil up to in the wilderness? He offered Jesus success without suffering and a crown without a cross. How alluring that must have been. Of course, that would have come at the cost of bowing the knee to the devil. In the end, Jesus rejected the lure.

Three years later, it was his own disciple, the man who would be the rock upon whom he would build his church, who was encouraging Jesus to pursue the crown without the cross. Peter wasn't intending to lead Jesus astray; he was only using human logic and seeking to look out for his friend. Which reminds me that even our Christian friends, pastors, and counselors can at times lead us away from God's path. They would, like Peter, do it unwittingly, but with real consequences. And we might be Peter for someone else, leading them astray without intending to do so. When we're thinking only human thoughts, we'll often counsel against the hard path, the way of suffering.

I've often counseled with people who were faced with a decision or dilemma where two roads diverged. One path was safe and comfortable and convenient. Or perhaps, like the last of Jesus' temptations in the wilderness, it promised quick riches, or instant gratification or success without suffering and only required a little compromising of their values. The other path was uncertain or difficult or inconvenient or uncomfortable. Most of us find that we have a natural tendency to want to help others take the easier and more convenient path, to say, "God wants you to be happy and not to suffer." This is true, but happiness and the avoidance suffering are not God's highest values. Sometimes, as pastor, I have to say, "I know this other path will be harder and more difficult, but it seems more consistent with the things that Jesus said and did."

Jesus' driving value was not what was easy, safe, or would make him happy. It was what would please God and accomplish God's purposes. He believed that his suffering, death, and resurrection would be used by God to redeem, save, and transform the world.

Yet the intensity of Jesus' response to Simon Peter points to just how hard pursuing this path was and all the harder when one of his closest disciples suggested this path was not necessary.

Take Up Your Own Cross

In response to Peter, Jesus explained that earthly power and glory were not on the path that he was taking—which meant that anyone who was sincere about following him would have to follow a road that would likely take them through suffering as well. He told the disciples plainly: "All who want to come after me must say no to themselves, take up their cross, and follow me" (Matthew 16:24).

The challenge is that we prefer self-fulfillment to self-denial. We would prefer to avoid sacrifice, and instead to play it safe without suffering or personal cost. And we're happy to follow Jesus provided it means blessings and bliss, hope and love, forgiveness and mercy. We want our religion to bless us, but we'd prefer it not ask anything too hard of us in return. This is true for me. I don't like self-denial; I'd prefer to have a convenient faith that doesn't demand too much sacrifice on my part.

Often our faith does provide blessings and joy, goodness and mercy. I feel like I've had more joy and blessings than I ever imagined, and certainly more than I deserve, and nearly all of it is somehow connected to my faith in Christ and the people he has brought into my life. But if my faith is authentically

Christian, it will lead me to give and live sacrificially, to yield my ego, to seek to live a life of servanthood, to serve others, and, at times, to make decisions I don't want to make in answer to his call.

The point is not pain and sacrifice for the sake of pain and sacrifice. During the conversation with Peter and the other disciples, Jesus went on to say: "All who want to save their lives will lose them. But all who lose their lives because of me will find them. Why would people gain the whole world but lose their lives?" (Matthew 16:25-26).

Here's what he was telling the disciples (not just the original twelve but all of us too): The fulfilled life we long for is found in self-denial, sacrifice, and in loving and serving God and others. Somehow, deep in our soul, we know this, even if we've never heard these words of Jesus. We have discovered that, in those times when we have given up ourselves for someone else, we find a joy that is deeper than the joy we find in self-indulgence. It is the kind of joy we cannot buy at the shopping mall. Something inside compels us to risk and sacrifice to do so. We are never more fully alive than when we are giving ourselves to help others. Maybe that's because, in those moments, we are living the way God always intended for us to be as human beings.

Jesus and Hurricane Harvey

In 2017 Hurricane Harvey struck the Gulf Coast of Texas, devastating parts of the Houston area and many other coastal towns. In the wake of the storm, people risked their lives by wading into the floodwater to rescue people they did not know. The news carried remarkable stories of what this looked like. Stephanie, a real estate agent, opened her apartment to families who needed a place to stay. Nick owned a semitruck that could go into places where the water was too deep for a car or a small truck. So Nick brought his big rig, and enlisted two other truckers who brought their trucks from two hundred miles away—that is, they brought the vehicles that represent their livelihoods—and together they carried more than one thousand people out of flooded areas and into safety.

Four bakers in the Houston area went into their bakery just ahead of the storm to bake bread for people. When Harvey struck Houston, they became trapped by the floodwaters. So they decided to use all the flour they had to make bread until they ran out. They worked for twenty hours straight. After the floodwaters subsided, they gave all their bread to rescue workers to deliver to others. The story of these bakers reminded me of Jesus multiplying the loaves to feed a hungry crowd. They didn't do it for money. They didn't sell what they made. They denied themselves and took up their cross.

As just one more example of what self-denial looks like, I saw the story of a guy who calls himself "Mattress Mack." His real name Jim McIngvale, and he owns furniture stores in Houston. When the floods drove people out of their homes and left them with no place to stay, Mattress Mack opened his stores as shelters. He sent out his delivery trucks to fetch people and bring them in under his roof to sleep on his furniture. More than four hundred people wound up sleeping in his showrooms. It didn't matter to Jim that his furniture that had been slept on could no longer be sold as new. He sacrificed his own interests on behalf of others.

These were ordinary, everyday people who denied themselves, took up their cross, and followed Jesus' path in seeking to love their neighbor.

The questions that arose from Peter's conversation with Jesus at Caesarea Philippi still call out to us today. Who do you say Jesus is?

Some, like the crowds of his own day, are willing to say, "He is a great prophet" or "He is an inspiring teacher."

But what about you? Are you willing, like Peter, to say that Jesus is your King, the one who represents God, the one to whom you pledge allegiance, the one whose words you seek to obey?

And if the answer is yes, are you willing to bear the cost of discipleship? Are you willing to deny yourself, take up your cross, and follow him?

If you answer yes, you'll discover the paradox of the gospel: it is in losing our lives, for Christ's sake, that we find life.

The Mount of Transfiguration

Before we end this chapter, I would like to visit one last experience in Simon Peter's life: his witness of Jesus' transfiguration.

Several years ago I spent a couple of days alone, hiking from Nazareth to Capernaum and beyond on the "Jesus Trail"— a marked system of trails in the Holy Land retracing the journeys of Jesus. I walked through woods, across hills and valleys. I spent this time reading the Gospels and praying. What struck me was just how much time Jesus must have had with his disciples that is glossed over in the Gospels. In the story of the Transfiguration as told by Matthew, we get a sense of this time spent walking with his disciples.

> *Six days later Jesus took Peter, James, and John his brother, and brought them to the top of a very high mountain. He was transformed in front of them. His face shone like the sun, and his clothes became as white as light.*
>
> *(Matthew 17:1-2)*

Six days the disciples spent walking and talking with Jesus following Peter's statement of faith and Jesus' words about self-denial and the cross. How I would love to have listened in on those conversations. Then Jesus took three of his disciples,

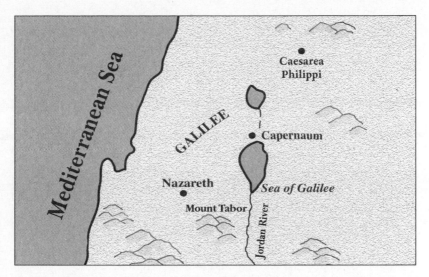

Peter, James and John, left the other nine behind, and hiked up a mountain. More conversations we're not privy to. But we do learn, in Matthew, Mark, and Luke, of the dramatic event that happened on the mountaintop.

Since the 200s, Christians have identified the mount Jesus ascended with Peter, James, and John as Mount Tabor. It is an unusual solitary protrusion, rising nearly two thousand feet in elevation from surrounding countryside. The large rounded mountain was on the main highway, the Via Maris that connected Africa to Asia. This was the road that connected Caesarea to the Galilee.

Mount Tabor is about fifty miles south by southwest of Caesarea and would have taken four or five days to reach, longer if Jesus stopped to minister and teach in the villages along the way. So Matthew's notation of, "Six days later…" gets us pretty close to Mount Tabor.

Special vans take pilgrims to the top of the mountain today on narrow switchbacks that wind back and forth up the steep hill. Once at the top, visitors can see the ruins of ancient churches that were built on top of this mountain starting in the 300s. The magnificent Church of the Transfiguration, built by

83

Mount Tabor is traditionally regarded as the mountain on which Jesus was transfigured. At the summit, the Church of the Transfiguration remembers this event.

the Franciscans in 1924 on the ruins of much older churches, marks the Transfiguration story.

Jesus didn't take all of the disciples to the top of the mountain, only Peter, James, and John—the "Rock" and the "Sons of Thunder" as he affectionately called them. On three occasions recorded in the Gospels, Jesus pulled these disciples apart from the others: when he went to raise the daughter of Jairus, the synagogue ruler, from the dead (Mark 5:21-43 and Luke 8:40-56); when he ascended the mountain for the Transfiguration; and in the Garden of Gethsemane when he was praying in agony. Was it a particular affection he had for them that caused Jesus to pull them aside, or was it to invest a bit more time in them and to give them a few more important experiences to prepare them for the leading roles they would play after his death?

Just before leaving Caesarea Philippi, Jesus had said, somewhat cryptically, "I assure you that some standing here won't die before they see the Human One coming in his kingdom" (Matthew 16:28). Now, on the mountain of transfiguration, Peter, James, and John were catching a glimpse—the Greek word in Matthew conveys the sense of a vision—of Jesus, the

Human One, "coming in his kingdom." They saw the glory of God on the face of Christ. Then suddenly they saw Moses and Elijah, Israel's greatest lawgiver and its greatest prophet, appear with Jesus, speaking to him. Finally, they hear the voice of God affirming that Jesus is in fact more than a lawgiver or prophet. He is God's dearly loved Son.

John's Gospel notes of Jesus, "We have seen his glory, glory like that of a father's only son, full of grace and truth" (John 1:14b), while Second Peter notes, "We witnessed his majesty with our own eyes. He received honor and glory from God the Father when a voice came to him from the magnificent glory, saying, 'This is my dearly loved Son, with whom I am well-pleased.' We ourselves heard this voice from heaven while we were with him on the holy mountain" (2 Peter 1:16b-19).

There's so much that could and should be said about this story, but our focus is on Peter, so let's see what Peter does when he sees this vision: "Peter reacted to all of this by saying to Jesus, 'Lord, it's good that we're here. If you want, I'll make three shrines: one for you, one for Moses, and one for Elijah.'" (Matthew 17:4). What an interesting thing to blurt out at that moment, and of course, it was Peter, not James or John, who said it. Mark offers an excuse for Peter, "He said this because he didn't know how to respond, for the three of them were terrified" (9:6).

I love this little line in part because it captures Peter's character. Jesus, Moses, and Elijah are standing before Peter—unbelievable! To be standing in the presence of these two towering figures of the Scriptures, both long dead—awe inspiring! And they are having a conversation with Jesus. What does Peter do? He interrupts them. He speaks up saying, in essence, "Jesus, lucky for you, you brought us! We'll get to work making tents for you if you'd like."

We've seen that Peter often speaks (and sometimes acts) before he thinks. He feels the need to say something and to *do something*. I appreciate this about Peter; I feel like I'm wired this way as well. I'm a type A who talks too much. I've been working, over the years, at doing a better job of listening and paying attention and taking in the experiences of life. But I still find that when I am seeing something amazing (a rainbow, a sunset, my granddaughter doing something sweet) my first reaction is to get out my phone and take a picture or video, then I feel compelled to post it on social media or send it to friends, and in the process, I miss the chance to simply take the experience in.

I wonder if Jesus didn't want to look at Peter and say, "Shhh. Peter, just listen and take this in. I brought you here to see this, not so that you could build us tents."

This is where, when I take the time to do it, journaling has helped me. It's led me to slow down and reflect upon the experiences of my day. It leads me to ask, "Where did I see God at work today? What did I learn today? What do I want to do differently tomorrow? And what am I thankful for today?"

By the way, before the Transfiguration is over, God himself tells Peter what he can do. God speaks from the cloud and says of Jesus, "Listen to him" (Matthew 17:5). That is the most important thing Peter can do—listen and pay attention to what Jesus says, since he will only be with Peter for a short while longer (remember, Simon's name means to hear or to listen). That is, of course, what we're meant to do. John captured this in speaking of Jesus as "the Word" that became flesh and lived among us.

On the way down the mountain, Jesus told his disciples that he was going to suffer. Jesus pointed the way, once more, to the cross and to the promise that his disciples would gain their lives by giving them up. Peter's vision of Jesus' transfiguration on the mountain didn't take away the reality that there was suffering ahead, but it allowed him to glimpse the glory that lay beyond it.

In many of my books I've included a prayer that is important in my life. It's often referred to as the "Wesley Covenant Prayer" and was used by early Methodists as a means of rededicating their lives to Christ—a way of recommitting themselves to listening to Jesus and following him even down the hard road. It includes an invitation, if need be, to put us to suffering. I pray some version of this every day. I thought you might find it meaningful to pray this prayer yourself.

I am no longer my own, but yours.
Put me to what you will, rank me with whom you will.
Put me to doing, put me to suffering.
Let me be employed by you or laid aside for you.
Exalted for you or brought low for you.
Let me be full, let me be empty.
Let me have all things, let me have nothing.
I freely and wholeheartedly yield all things to your pleasure and disposal.[1]

4

"I WILL NOT DENY YOU"

Then Jesus said to them, "You will all become deserters because of me this night; for it is written,

> *'I will strike the shepherd,
>   and the sheep of the flock will be scattered.'*

But after I am raised up, I will go ahead of you to Galilee." Peter said to him, "Though all become deserters because of you, I will never desert you." Jesus said to him, "Truly I tell you, this very night, before the cock crows, you will deny me three times." Peter said to him, "Even though I must die with you, I will not deny you." And so said all the disciples.

(Matthew 26:31-35 NRSV)

In the last chapter we traveled with Jesus and his disciples to the northernmost point in their journeys, in Caesarea Philippi. Jesus had just announced to his disciples that he would be put to death in Jerusalem. This is a hinge point in the story. From there on, Jesus was preparing himself—and his disciples—for his death. On the Mount of Transfiguration, Peter, James, and John glimpsed Jesus' glory, but they would not truly comprehend it until after Jesus' death and resurrection. Jesus' arrest, trial, and crucifixion still lay ahead. In this chapter, we'll focus on the events leading up to Jesus' death, especially those involving Peter the evening of the Last Supper.

From Transfiguration to the Upper Room

Fully one-fourth of Matthew's Gospel—seven of the twenty-eight chapters—is about the final week of Jesus' life, climaxing in his death and resurrection. Jesus lived thirty-three years, but the focus comes down to the last week of his life. In the rest of this chapter, we'll focus on Maundy Thursday and Good Friday, but I'd like to begin with a very brief rundown of the journey from the Mount of Transfiguration to Jerusalem.

After coming down the Mount of Transfiguration, Jesus, Peter, and the other disciples made the twenty-mile journey back to Capernaum, the home base of Jesus' ministry. The rest of Matthew 17 and 18 takes place in and around Capernaum. In Matthew 19, the disciples begin the one-hundred-mile journey to Jerusalem, stopping first in Jericho, then entering Jerusalem from the east, descending the Mount of Olives

As they approached the Holy City, word spread that Jesus was coming. A crowd brought branches—leafy branches, which John tells us were palm branches—and waved them as Jesus came down the Mount of Olives. This was how the Jews in the days of the Maccabees celebrated the victory of the rebels. Palm branches had become a sign of Jewish victory. The people began to hail Jesus as the "son of David" and shouted "Hosanna," a cry of acclamation that means, "Deliver us now!" It was this kind of display that Jesus had previously tamped down, asking his disciples not to tell anyone that he was the Messiah. But now he accepted it, knowing it would lead to his arrest later that week. Upon entering the city, Jesus turned over the tables of the money changers and drove out the merchants from the temple courts, infuriating the religious leadership and sealing his fate.

Each day that week, Jesus and his disciples returned to the temple where Jesus taught the crowds. There was an intensity about his words, and at times they included barbed criticism of the religious leaders. I suspect you could cut the tension with a knife, given that Jesus was teaching and critiquing the religious leadership, and calling for repentance, right in the center of their power.

On Thursday morning of that week, Luke tells us that Jesus sent Peter and John into town (they stayed nights on the Mount of Olives) to prepare the Passover meal for the disciples. They purchased the slaughtered Passover lamb, found a guest room Jesus had made arrangements for, had the lamb roasted and the other elements of the meal readied, and had the meal set up for the upper room. I wonder if Peter felt put-upon that, rather than spending the day with Jesus, he was sent to do the ordinary task of preparing for the meal, a meal whose true import he did not yet understand. Peter, John, and the owner of the house ensured that everything was ready for what we know as the Last Supper.

Washing Feet and True Greatness

When the disciples walked into the upper room to share this Passover meal, they did not yet realize that it would be Jesus' last meal before his execution. As they entered the room, Jesus and the disciples would have removed their sandals, leaving them by the door. This is still the custom in much of the world. Why did people remove their shoes at the door? The sole of the shoe tracked in dirt. In the ancient Near East, people didn't have furniture as we think of it. They sat on mats or pillows *on the floor.* They ate at low tables while reclining on cushions *on the floor.* They slept on mats, *on the floor.* Taking off one's shoes at the door reflected cleanliness and good manners, avoiding carrying dirt into living areas. (It turns out they may have been on to something. Researchers at the University of Houston found that 39 percent of shoes they studied carried the Clostridium difficile bacteria spores—C. Diff—that can cause diarrhea and even death.[4])

But after people took off their sandals, their feet were still dusty, and so there was a custom of providing water, a basin, and a towel to rinse off one's feet as one entered a house. If there was a household servant this might be part of their job, to rinse and dry each person's feet as they entered the home. But if there was no servant, then a pitcher of water, a basin, and towel were left by the door for those who entered to wash their own feet. This was not only a way of ensuring cleanliness, it was an act of kindness for those who had "put in their steps" wearing sandals on the dusty roads. On this night, the host had the pitcher of water, basin, and towel in the upper room for Jesus and his disciples.

Yet as the disciples walked in, none of them stopped to wash their feet. I've always wondered why. I imagine it was because each was afraid that if he stopped to wash his own feet, he knew Jesus would expect him to take the role of the servant and wash the feet of those who followed him into the room. None would want to get stuck in such a demeaning role.

To the disciples' astonishment and embarrassment, shortly after they were seated, Jesus went and retrieved the pitcher, towel, and basin, and he assumed the role of the servant. He began washing the disciples' feet. The discomfort in the room was palpable. There was something very wrong with this picture. Jesus was their rabbi, their master, the one they believed was the Messiah. He should not be washing their feet. But no one spoke up.

That very evening, according to Luke's account of the Last Supper, they had been debating, quietly so Jesus wouldn't hear them, which of them would be Jesus' right hand as he took power (they still did not get it, that Jesus was going to die). Jesus knew what they were discussing. And the message he was giving them by silently washing their feet was deafening.

When Jesus came to Simon, it was the Rock who spoke up. He, alone, said to Jesus, "No! You will never wash my feet!" (John 13:8). This wasn't anger or obstinacy but an appropriate sense that it was he who should have washed Jesus' feet, not the other way around. Peter had walked past that basin when he walked in the door, just like the others. But now he felt a profound sense of embarrassment, both that he had not stopped to do this, and that Jesus was ready to wash his feet.

Have you ever seen someone who needed a little help, but you passed on the chance, only to feel embarrassed when the person next to you chose to help? It may have been giving up a seat on the subway to someone who was older. It could have been helping someone get luggage into, or out of, the overhead bin on an airplane. Maybe it was someone homeless on the streets whom you passed by. You know that feeling of embarrassment, that you thought about doing the kind and compassionate thing and didn't, only to watch someone else do it instinctively. I am guessing all twelve of the disciples were feeling this on this night. The possible exception is Judas Iscariot, who, it appears, was already frustrated that Jesus was not doing enough to seize power and become the kind of Messiah he had been hoping for as he followed Jesus. If this was the case, Jesus' washing the disciples feet may have been one more sign of weakness to him.

In any case, it was only Simon who spoke up, only Simon who said, "This is not right." But Jesus was going to make sure Peter took the medicine too. He wanted them all to remember the lesson, so Jesus said, "Unless I wash you, you won't have a place with me" (John 13:8). Unless you allow me to serve you in this way, Jesus was saying, you really don't get it. You cannot share in the kingdom that I am proclaiming.

I love Peter's response, as it indicates both his passion and his continuing confusion. "Lord, not only my feet but also my hands and my head!" (13:9). Suddenly, he was all in. That was Peter being Peter. And I imagine Jesus was smiling when he replied that those who have had a bath need just their feet washed.

In assuming the role of a servant, Jesus was teaching once more. He attempted to help Peter and the disciples understand who he was, and what he demanded of them (and us). After he put away the basin of water and the towel, he told them, "Do you know what I've done for you? You call me 'Teacher' and 'Lord,' and you speak correctly, because I am. If I, your Lord and teacher, have washed your feet, you too must wash each other's feet. I have given you an example: Just as I have done, you also must do" (13:12-15). The disciples would never forget this lesson.

For us, of course, the lesson isn't really about washing feet. That's not a routine task in our culture, although some churches still practice foot washing as a symbolic act. Jesus' lesson was much deeper, and once again Peter was the foil to let Jesus teach it. As Jesus put it in Luke's Gospel, "The greatest among you must become like a person of lower status and the leader like a servant" (Luke 22:26).

Robert Greenleaf coined the phrase *servant leadership* in 1970, and he did a lot to spread the idea. But the concept originated with Jesus nearly two thousand years earlier. How are you at servant leadership? What does that look like in your life? If you are in leadership in a company or an organization, how are you also a servant? Where do others see that in your actions?

Greenleaf was a management leadership guru. But servant leadership really is a key to success in almost anything in life. Marriages are successful when two people act as servants toward each other. They wake up each morning and recognize that part of their job is to bless their partner, encourage them, and build them up. It involves ministering to each other. And it only works when both people share that attitude, giving as well as receiving.

That's really what the wedding vow to "cherish" means—in sickness and in health, for as long as they both shall live.

Servanthood is a key to success in business too. Almost every business, after all, has customers whom they serve. When businesses focus on how to serve their customers really well, the financial side tends to take care of itself. Danny O'Neil, a member of the church I serve, started and owns a business called The Roasterie. Some have described it as the best coffee production house in the United States. They roast all kinds of amazing coffees and coffee blends. I once asked Danny to describe the keys to The Roasterie's success. Servant leadership was the first thing he mentioned. He said that doing the best job possible of serving his customers has always been his focus, going back to the days when he was the company's only employee. There is one thing, he added, that will lead to an employee's firing on the spot: if someone says, "That's not my job!" Everyone must be willing to serve.

In essence, this is what Jesus was teaching Peter and the others that night by washing their feet and telling them to serve one another.

By the sixth century AD, the popes in Rome were among the most powerful people in the world. Such awesome power corrupted some of them. Then in 590, Pope Gregory I became the leader of the church. I love how he defined his role: to be the servant of the servants of God. This is still how the popes sign certain documents. I wonder how our lives might change if we each saw this as our mission—that we are servants of others, servants of our mates, servants of our customers, servants of our fellow employees, and servants of the servants of God.

You Will All Become Deserters

Following the foot washing, Jesus and the disciples broke bread together, sharing the Passover seder.* John devotes

---

* In John's Gospel it is not the Passover seder, but in Matthew, Mark, and Luke it is the seder meal. John writes that Jesus was crucified on the day of preparation as the Passover lambs were being sacrificed.

five chapters to describing all that Jesus taught that night. The Synoptic Gospels have just a fraction of that. Our aim in this book is to explore the material that specifically focuses on Simon Peter. So our focus will be on the predictions Jesus made that night that the disciples would desert him. Here's what Matthew records:

> Then Jesus said to them, "You will all become deserters because of me this night; for it is written,
>
> > 'I will strike the shepherd,
> > and the sheep of the flock will be scattered.'
>
> But after I am raised up, I will go ahead of you to Galilee." Peter said to him, "Though all become deserters because of you, I will never desert you." Jesus said to him, "Truly I tell you, this very night, before the cock crows, you will deny me three times." Peter said to him, "Even though I must die with you, I will not deny you." And so said all the disciples.
>
> (Matthew 26:31-35 NRSV)

Judas had already sold Jesus out for thirty pieces of silver; he planned to betray him that very night, leading the temple guard to the place where Jesus and the disciples had been staying on the Mount of Olives each night that week. But the others were oblivious to Judas's plans. They knew the tension was mounting between the religious authorities and Jesus, but they were not at all prepared for what Judas was setting in motion.

Once again, it was Peter, the Rock, who spoke up first and most forcefully. I love how Matthew records his words. In essence he says, "Even if these others abandon you, I will never do that, ever." Bold words from the man who would deny Jesus three times before the night was out. I believe Peter sincerely meant what he said. But when it came down to the moment when he himself might be arrested, he was overcome by fear. Bold and courageous, fearful and flawed. That was Peter.

Jesus knew Peter's flaws. We have seen them, too, throughout the Gospel story. And so Jesus told him something that came to haunt him: "Truly I tell you, this very night, before the cock crows, you will deny me three times" (Matthew 26:34 NRSV). These must have been painful words for Peter to hear, being singled out by Jesus and told of his impending failure of nerve. He repeated his promise of loyalty: "Even though I must die with you, I will not deny you" (Matthew 26:35 NRSV).

To the Garden, with a Sword

Of course, we know from the Gospel story that Jesus was right about Peter. But before we get to what Peter did in the wee hours of the morning, it's worth taking a moment to review what happened between the Last Supper and Peter's denial, because those events shed some additional light on Peter's character and actions.

After finishing their Passover meal, the disciples sang a hymn. Already in the time of Jesus the tradition was to say or sing certain Psalms at the Passover, ending with Psalm 118—you might find it interesting to read the words of that Psalm. Jesus and the disciples left the upper room, crossed the Kidron Valley, and went to pray in the garden of Gethsemane. Jesus asked eight of the disciples to stay and pray near the entrance to the garden. Then he took Peter, James, and John with him a bit farther into the garden, wanting them nearby. Perhaps he was hoping they would watch him, see his agony, and maybe even overhear his prayers—which apparently they did, as we have a record of Jesus' prayer and his state of mind, likely from their memory of what they saw. Then he went a bit farther still and found a place where he prayed and agonized with such intensity that, as the Gospel account tells us, he sweat drops of blood. He asked of God: "My Father, if it's possible, take this cup of suffering away from me. However—not what I want but what you want" (Matthew 26:39).

97

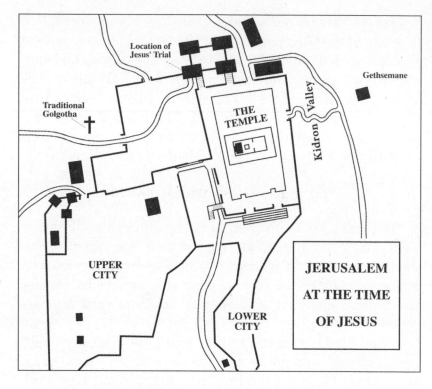

Jesus came back to check on Peter, James, and John, perhaps needing to know that they were with him, that he could draw strength from them. But he found them asleep. Matthew records, "[Jesus] said to Peter, 'Couldn't you stay alert one hour with me? Stay alert and pray so that you won't give in to temptation. The spirit is eager, but the flesh is weak'" (vv. 40-41). This happened two more times, and each time Jesus had to wake the disciples.

It is easy for me to relate to this part of Peter's story. All of us, at one time or another, have probably fallen asleep in church even though we were doing our best to stay awake. I often work late at night, and I was up around 1 a.m. one night working on a sermon on this very text. I was sitting at my computer, with my Bible beside me and a Bible commentary on my lap, and I fell asleep. When I woke up twenty minutes later, I had to erase

At this olive grove in Gethsemane, the church remembers Peter, James, and John sleeping while Jesus prayed before his arrest. The gravel path leads to the oldest and largest tree in the garden, which some believe was alive in the time of Christ.

five pages of the letter *j* that I had typed because I had nodded off with my finger on that key. I couldn't help but think of Jesus' stinging words to Peter: "Couldn't you stay alert one hour with me?"

After the third time that Jesus awakened his sleeping disciples, they saw the torches coming toward them. The torches were carried by armed members of the temple guard, accompanied by Judas Iscariot as well as some of the religious authorities. A crowd followed with swords and clubs. Judas identified Jesus for the authorities by kissing him on the cheek.

Then, as John's Gospel tells it, Peter sprang into action, drawing the sword he was carrying and striking one of the men who had come to arrest Jesus, a servant of the high priest whose name was Malchus. He cut off a piece of his right ear.

99

Note once more, Peter was the only one of the Twelve to act. His act of courage was an attempt to do precisely what he had promised Jesus, to stay with Jesus rather than desert him. But it also could have gotten all the other disciples, and Jesus, killed on the spot, ending the important work Jesus had done to mentor and to pour into them over the preceding three years. They were the ones Jesus was counting on to carry on his work.

Jesus turned to Simon Peter and said, "Put the sword back into its place. All those who use the sword will die by the sword. "Or do you think that I'm not able to ask my Father and he will send to me more than twelve battle groups of angels right away? (v. 53). Once more Simon is acting boldly, trying to protect Jesus' honor, and once again, Jesus corrects Simon.

Luke tells us that Jesus picked up Malchus's severed ear, put it back in its place, and healed him (Luke 22:51). Jesus healed the servant of an enemy, even as his enemies were attempting to arrest him. And then Jesus pleaded for his disciples. He said to the temple authorities, "If you are looking for me, then let these people go." (John 18:8) As Jesus was being led away, the disciples fled in fear. They deserted Jesus—just as he had said they would.

"I Don't Know Him"

The temple officials took Jesus back across the Kidron Valley and made their way to the house of the high priest, Caiaphas. In the place Christians have marked as Caiaphas's home, a modern church sits atop the ruins of much more ancient churches. The church, built in 1931 by the Augustinians, is called St. Peter in Gallicantu (*gallicantu* is the Latin word for cock-crow). As early as the 300s, perhaps before, Christians have come to this place remembering Jesus' arrest and Peter's denial.

From the Church of St. Peter in Gallicantu, the garden of Gethsemane and the Mount of Olives can be seen to the east. To the north is the Temple Mount. To the south is the Hinnom

In the courtyard of the Church of St. Peter in Gallicantu, this sculpture reminds pilgrims of Peter's threefold denial of Jesus.

Valley. (You can see the traditional location of the Potter's Field where Judas Iscariot was said to have hung himself after he was filled with remorse for betraying Jesus.)

An ancient stairway, thought to be from the Roman era, leads up from the Kidron Valley to the site and is thought to be the path along which Jesus would have been led as he was brought to Caiaphas's palace for trial. It used to be that pilgrims could remove their shoes and walk up the path, one's feet touching the stones on which Jesus' feet trod on his way to trial. All but the top two or three steps are now fenced off.

Beneath the church are ancient cisterns thought to have been used as a prison for those awaiting trial. There a particular pit is associated with Jesus' detainment. Another cistern is often associated with Peter's arrest and detainment in Acts 5:17-42. The church's archaeological remains, as well as its architecture

101

and art, take visitors to that night of the arrest, trial, and betrayal of Jesus, allowing you to step into the story. Many find it very powerful.

It was late at night when Jesus was taken by the guards across the Kidron Valley and up to the high priest's house. The Jewish ruling council, the Sanhedrin, was hastily called together. Though the other disciples had fled, Peter and John followed in the darkness, unwilling to desert Jesus. Upon arriving at the house, they found a small crowd gathered in the courtyard. A fire was lit by which those present were warming themselves. Peter and John took a risk and joined the crowd, hoping they would not be recognized.

We often remember Peter for his denial of Jesus that night, but consider the courage it took to step onto the courtyard of the high priest's home, where the temple guards who had just arrested Jesus sauntered around the fire. Peter had just wielded a sword against the servant of the high priest. It seems there was a high likelihood someone who was at the arrest would recognize Peter and either arrest him or kill him on the spot. Yet Peter stepped into the courtyard, unwilling to abandon Jesus.

While Jesus was on trial inside the home, Peter was about to face his own kind of trial. In the firelight, a servant-woman, likely a woman who had been among the crowd at the arrest, spoke up saying, "You were also with Jesus the Galilean" (Matthew 26:69). Matthew notes, "But he denied it in front of all of them, saying, 'I don't know what you are talking about'" (v. 70).

Matthew continues, "When he went over to the gate, another woman saw him and said to those who were there, 'This man was with Jesus, the man from Nazareth'" (v. 71). Once more Peter denied being a disciple of Jesus saying, "I don't know the man" (v. 72).

Luke tells us that another hour passed. John notes that Peter was warming himself by the fire when a man approached Peter (John tells us it was a relative of the man whose ear Peter had sliced off). He, too, asked whether it was Peter who was in the garden with Jesus. Listen to how Matthew tells what happened next:

> *He began to curse, and he swore an oath, "I do not know the man!" At that moment the cock crowed. Then Peter remembered what Jesus had said: "Before the cock crows, you will deny me three times." And he went out and wept bitterly.*
>
> *(Matthew 26:74-75 NRSV)*

This story engenders such pathos. Peter demonstrated a courage and faithfulness to Jesus that none of the other disciples could muster up. He sought to defend Jesus with the sword, then followed all the way to the courtyard, seeking to fulfill his promise to Jesus that "Even though I must die with you, I will not deny you" (v. 35). But in the end, fear led the Rock to curse and swear and to deny even knowing Jesus, not once, but three times. It is not hard to imagine Peter fleeing into the darkness following his last denial, weeping uncontrollably.

Inspiring Followers by Confessing Failures

I want to return to an idea I mentioned in the introduction. The Gospels were all written after Peter's death. As we'll learn in the final chapter of this book, Peter died courageously, having spent the last thirty-five years of his life boldly proclaiming Christ. Why then, when the various Gospel writers were recording his part in Jesus' story, would they include Peter's greatest failure as a disciple? And while the Gospels don't contain all the same stories, this is the one story about Peter that all four Gospels record—his failure of nerve and his denial of Christ at Jesus' trial. Typically, following the death of revered figures, their shortcomings and failures are minimized, while their positive attributes and saintly stories are repeated and accentuated. So why would a church that loves Peter retell this story of Peter's denial?

I'm convinced that they told this story about Peter because Peter himself insisted on telling it over and over again. It became so associated with Peter and his ministry that not to tell the story would have been a great disservice.

What I think Peter and the Gospel writers wanted us to see in this story is that we have all, like Peter, denied Jesus by our thoughts, our words, or our deeds, both by what we have done and by what we should have done but didn't. We have all lived at times in ways that were inconsistent with our pledge to follow Christ. We've mistreated others. We've joined in the taunting, teasing, or gossip that hurt others. We've given in to materialism or idolatry or lust. For all of us, there have been moments when our witness or example was needed, but we remained silent and did nothing.

Paul Plummer was working at the IGA grocery store in St. Joseph, Missouri, in 1933 when a crowd of as many as seven thousand of his friends and neighbors and a host of others gathered around the town's jailhouse. They had come for Lloyd Warner, a nineteen-year-old black man accused of raping a twenty-one-year-old white woman. While interrogated he confessed, but later recanted his confession. The young woman was certain it was Warner, then not certain, then certain again. Warner was to be tried, but the crowd, or at least the twelve ringleaders, didn't want to wait for the criminal justice system.

Plummer rushed out and stood at the edge of the crowd, watching to see what would happen next. After law enforcement attempted to prevent Warner's abduction, the ringleaders were taken to Warner, who was dragged out of the courthouse, beaten severely, then hung. Not satisfied with his hanging, they drenched his body in gasoline and lit him on fire. As I write these words, I'm looking at a photograph of white men proudly standing over the still smoldering body of Lloyd Warner.

Plummer told of the experience thirty years later in a sermon he was preaching as the lay leader of the Frankfort Methodist Church. His sermon was called, "Standing on the Edge of the

Crowd." He described the silence of the crowd. Despite the uncertain circumstances of his confession or the uncertain identification of the man by the victim of the rape, and despite the lack of a trial meant to ensure justice, these men felt justified in their brutality, and no one in the crowd spoke up to protest—a crowd filled with churchgoing Christians. Plummer, a gentle giant of a man, described thirty years of remorse and shame for not having spoken up.

Would you have spoken up? Enough people felt remorse about Warner's death that his was the last lynching ever recorded in St. Joseph, Missouri. Yet none of them spoke up at the time.

Few people are still alive who stood by at a lynching, but we've all been Paul Plummer at some point in our lives. We've been afraid to speak up in the face of injustice or to stand up to a bully or to work to resist what was evil. And in a hundred other ways we've denied Jesus by our thoughts, words, or deeds.

I wonder how you have denied him. Every week in my own life, there is some place or some time when I have thoughts that are not fitting for a Christian or I say something that I should not have said or do something I should not have done. Each Sunday, during our time in worship of silent confessional prayer, I know I need to ask for forgiveness for denying Jesus. Peter's story is for all of us. Peter showed us that denying Jesus is part of our all-too-human experience as disciples.

But Peter's story also shows us that we need not be defined by our failures. God does not define us by the worst thing we ever did. Jesus makes amazing use of flawed disciples. He continually invites us back, forgives us, and restores us. Sometimes he uses us even more profoundly, not merely in spite of our flaws and failures but because of them. Jesus is the Lord of the second chance. If the disciple who denied knowing Jesus could become the Rock on which the church was built, there is hope for us too. Simon Peter wasn't afraid to talk about his shortcomings as a way to help others learn, grow, and find grace. He knew that every person who commits to follow Jesus would fall short.

105

On many occasions I have sat in my office with people who were sobbing, as Peter did, because they had done something for which they were horribly ashamed. I have reminded them of this story of Peter. He, too, wept in guilt, sorrow, and shame. But I also remind them our worst failure might very well be something that God can use in our witness in the future. Telling the stories of how we have failed can actually encourage people and help them find hope. This is what happened with Peter, who told this story again and again. And it is the impact this story continues to have on readers of the Gospels today.

I have discovered that the stories my congregation finds most compelling about me are not the stories where I got it right. It is the times I'm willing to confess that I blew it and needed God's grace. God uses our shortcomings and failures.

My friend Jorge Acevedo pastors a large United Methodist Church in Florida. He tells the story of how his church's addiction ministries began as a result of the instructions Jorge was giving before Communion during a worship service, when he admitted that he had struggled with alcoholism. During his invitation to the Lord's Supper he said, "So, if you struggle with alcohol like I do, then please know that this is a safe table for you." He told me, "What I didn't even realize was that I was outing myself as a person in recovery that day. Some people were shocked when I said it. But a funny thing happened. Everyone in church that day who was an alcoholic or who struggled with some kind of addiction went out and found their friends who struggled with the same issues and told them, 'You've got to come to church with me. My pastor knows what it's like to struggle with addiction.'" Today, more than one thousand people gather every week at one of the five campuses of Grace Church to participate in their 12-Step programs. In fact, their ministry is one of the largest recovery programs in the country. And it started because the pastor was willing to tell a story of his failings and his struggles.

Pastor Jorge did what I believe Peter spent years doing as the Rock shared the story of his denial of Jesus: he revealed his own weakness in order to strengthen and encourage others. That is another expression of servant leadership.

We're called to be servant leaders. With some regularity, we blow it. But in the next chapter, we'll see how Jesus restored Peter, just as he restores us. And ultimately, he can use our failures and shortcomings to illuminate the path for others. That is Simon Peter's story. Will it be yours?

Lord, let me be your servant by serving others. As my guide, let me remember the way you humbly washed your disciples' feet. Grant me the faith and the courage, in spite of my failings and my denials, to follow you wherever you call me to go. Amen.

5

FROM COWARDICE
TO COURAGE

Jesus said to them, "Come and have breakfast."...

*When they finished eating, Jesus asked Simon
Peter, "Simon son of John, do you love me more
than these?"*

Simon replied, "Yes, Lord, you know I love you."

*Jesus said to him, "Feed my lambs." Jesus asked
a second time, "Simon son of John, do you love
me?"*

Simon replied, "Yes, Lord, you know I love you."

*Jesus said to him, "Take care of my sheep." He
asked a third time, "Simon son of John, do you
love me?"*

> *Peter was sad that Jesus asked him a third time,*
> *"Do you love me?" He replied, "Lord, you know*
> *everything; you know I love you."*
>
> *Jesus said to him, "Feed my sheep."*
>
> (John 21:12, 15-17)

When last we saw Simon Peter, it was the worst night of his life. He watched as his teacher and friend was arrested. Following at a distance, he entered the courtyard of the high priest's home. There, several people recognized him as a follower of Jesus, but when confronted by them, Simon denied knowing Jesus.

Meanwhile, inside the house of the high priest that night, Jesus was on trial on charges of blasphemy. Before the night was out, the Jewish ruling council sentenced Jesus to death. At dawn, Jesus was sent to the Roman governor Pontius Pilate, whose Jerusalem headquarters was a ten-minute walk from the high priest's house, within what is today the Old City of Jerusalem. Pilate, though unconvinced of Jesus' guilt, wished to satisfy the religious leaders and the crowd that had gathered outside his headquarters. He sentenced Jesus to be beaten, then crucified on Calvary. By 9 a.m., Jesus was stretched out upon the cross, affixed to it, and then the cross was raised. There he would hang, slowly dying one of the most cruel and inhumane deaths invented by mortals. I've explored the crucifixion of Christ in detail in other books.* For our purposes I'd like to focus on what was happening to the disciples, particularly Peter, as Jesus was crucified.

Matthew tells us that on that Friday morning, Judas, feeling great remorse, returned the thirty pieces of silver he had been paid to betray Jesus, then hung himself. John's Gospel tells us that John alone among the remaining disciples had the courage to stand with Mary, the mother of Jesus, and Mary Magdalene,

---

* See *24 Hours That Changed the World* (Nashville: Abingdon, 2010); *Final Words From the Cross* (Nashville: Abingdon, 2011); and *The Way: Walking in the Footsteps of Jesus* (Nashville:Abingdon, 2012).

at the foot of the cross. There they watched as Jesus slowly died. Other women, Matthew tells us, including the mother of the apostles James and John, watched from a distance. None of the Gospels tell us where Peter or the other nine disciples were on that terrible day.

The Rock upon whom Jesus declared he would build his church was in hiding. Might he have watched from a distance? Perhaps. But it's possible he couldn't stand to watch and instead remained hiding in grief, remorse, and shame.

Peter was not there to hear Jesus' final words. He was not there when Jesus was taken down from the cross. Peter was not there as Joseph of Arimathea and Nicodemus prepared Jesus' body for burial and laid him in the tomb. He was not there as the stone was rolled in front of the mouth of tomb, sealing Jesus' body in the grave.

As night fell, I imagine Simon Peter and the others gathered in the upper room, where they would remain until Easter evening. I imagine they had gathered at the home where they finally come back into the story on Easter morning. John tells us that on Easter, "the disciples were behind closed doors because they were afraid of the Jewish authorities" (20:19). In my mind, I picture the scene there following the Crucifixion resembling one I've experienced on many occasions when I've come to the home of a family who just lost a loved one to a tragic accident, suicide, or murder. People sit in silence, quietly crying. With each new person who walks in the door there are hugs and more tears. Food is brought in by friends, not knowing what else to do to comfort the people they love, but no one feels like eating. From time to time someone says, "Do you remember when…" which breaks the silence for a moment, but inevitably leads to more tears. The only difference I picture between these contemporary scenes and that of the disciples is the fear the disciples would have felt knowing that the temple guard or the Romans could be coming to arrest them as well.

Had the Crucifixion been the end of Jesus' story, it surely would have been the end of Peter's story too. Most likely he would have returned to Galilee and his fishing business. Or, if his life continued to be in danger from the religious leaders or the Romans, he may have fled to another country and assumed a new identity. Either way, chances are that Peter would have been lost to history.

We know, of course, that the cross wasn't the end of Peter's story, and that he went on to become the rock Jesus predicted he would be. What happened to transform Peter, moving him from cowardice to unshakable courage? What was it that gave him the boldness to preach and teach to the multitudes of Jerusalem and beyond that Jesus was the Messiah? That is what we will explore in the rest of this chapter.

"Especially Peter"

On Sunday morning, less than forty-eight hours after Jesus' crucifixion, women went to Jesus' tomb. He had been hastily buried before the Sabbath began at sunset on Friday. Now that the Sabbath was over, they hoped to complete the burial preparations using spices and oils. The number and names of the women differ in the various Gospel accounts, but they all agree that Mary Magdalene was there. She was the woman out of whom Jesus had cast multiple demons, the same woman who courageously stood with Jesus' mother at the foot of the cross.

She arrived and found the large stone rolled away. Again, the Gospels differ on the details, telling the story in slightly different ways. But they agree that there was at least one young man in a white robe at the tomb and that the tomb was empty.

In Mark, the earliest of the Gospels to be written, the young man says to the very frightened women,

> *"You are looking for Jesus of Nazareth, who was crucified. He has been raised. He isn't here. Look, here's*

the place where they laid him. Go, tell his disciples,
especially Peter, that he is going ahead of you into
Galilee. You will see him there, just as he told you."

(Mark 16:6-7)

I love that, "Go, tell his disciples, especially Peter." Why *especially* Peter? What would it have meant to Peter that the messenger of God had specifically singled him out, asking him to go to Galilee to meet the risen Jesus? I think for Peter it would have meant the hope that, despite his denial of Jesus, he was still wanted, needed, and loved. I think it would have meant that Jesus might well forgive him. And it would have been a sign that there was more for him to do. He might still be the Rock upon which Jesus' church would be built.

When I read this text and share it with my congregation, I remind them of Peter's denial, and how these words, "especially Peter," are tied to that. Then I remind them that, because of the grace of Christ who forgives our own denials of Jesus, we might put our name in the place of Peter's, as if the words of hope are for, "especially Susan" or "especially Stephen" or "especially Olivia" or "especially Adam." Or especially *you*. Again, Jesus knows your shortcomings, failures, and denials, and he offers hope and grace especially to you.

Looking at the other Easter accounts, we find in Luke's Gospel that, just after discovering that the tomb is empty, Mary and the other women ran to the place where the disciples were hiding. They told the disciples about the stone and the empty tomb, and the young men in white (Luke and John tell us there were two young men, not one as in Mark and Matthew).

Luke records the response of the disciples, and especially Peter:

Their words struck the apostles as nonsense, and they
didn't believe the women. But Peter ran to the tomb.
When he bent over to look inside, he saw only the linen

> *cloth. Then he returned home, wondering what had happened.*
>
> *(Luke 24:11-12)*

Why did Peter run to the tomb? In John's account, it was both Peter and John who ran to the tomb while the other disciples remained in hiding. John outran Peter (I love that John felt the need to include this detail in his Gospel!), but it was Peter who entered the tomb first. In both Luke and John, Peter is the first, after the women, to enter the empty tomb. He sees the grave clothes lying there. But he is not yet convinced that Christ is risen, despite the testimony of the women, and despite the fact that Jesus had, beginning on the Mount of Transfiguration, told him he would rise.

As an aside, we are meant to notice that it was a woman, Mary of Magdala, who was the first to see the resurrected Christ. Mary Magdalene who helped financially support the mission of Jesus and the apostles, who had been delivered from demons, who had the courage to stand at the cross as Jesus died, who accompanied his body to the grave—it was this Mary that God gave the privilege of being the first to learn that Jesus was alive. She was the first to see Jesus after his resurrection. And she was the first to proclaim Easter to others.

Yet Simon Peter remains unconvinced that Jesus has in fact been raised. The alternative to Mary's account, for Peter, would have meant someone had opened the tomb and removed Jesus' body, quite likely to desecrate it. At this point he was simply not sure what to think.

Luke tells us that two followers of Jesus, Cleopas and an anonymous disciple, were walking to Emmaus with their faces "downcast." (Some have suggested the anonymous disciple was Cleopas's wife, and that his wife was the "Mary, the wife of Clopas" in John 19:25 who was at the Crucifixion.) They had already heard that the tomb had been found empty and that the women had claimed to have seen Christ risen. But their faces were downcast because, on that first Easter afternoon, they, like Peter, did not believe the report of the women that Jesus had been raised. Instead, they must have been convinced that the body of Jesus had been taken—one final attempt to discredit and humiliate him.

Jesus approached these two disciples while they were walking to Emmaus, but appeared as a stranger, listening to them, then explaining how the Messiah had to die. That afternoon, as the stranger gave thanks and broke bread at a meal (as Jesus had done many times with his disciples and friends), their eyes were opened and they could see the stranger was Jesus. Just then he disappeared from their sight. They rushed back to tell the disciples, at which point the disciples told them, "Jesus appeared to Simon!"

We have no record of this appearance to Peter—when it happened and what Jesus said to him. But we know of it not only from Luke 24 but also from the Apostle Paul in 1 Corinthians 15:5, as he is describing the appearances of the risen Christ: "He appeared to Cephas [Peter], then to the Twelve." It is worth nothing that Paul wrote 1 Corinthians years before any of the Gospels were written. While we know nothing else about this visit, a private conversation Jesus had with Peter, it is clear that Jesus intentionally went looking for Simon Peter that afternoon. He needed Peter to know that he was, in fact, alive.

The Gospels record several different episodes when the resurrected Jesus appeared to his disciples. (1) He appears to the women early Easter morning (Matthew 28:8-10; in John 20:10-18 he only appears to Mary Magdalene). (2) That afternoon, he appears to the two disciples walking to Emmaus (Cleopas and an unnamed disciple, possibly his wife; Luke 24:13-35). (3) Just before or after this, he appears to Simon Peter (Luke 24:34). (4) On Easter evening he appears to the disciples (Luke 24:36-49; John 20:19-23). (5) A week later he appeared to them, along with Thomas who was missing on Easter (John 20:24-29). (6) Matthew and Luke record the giving of the Great Commission just before Christ's ascension, though Matthew has this occur in Galilee while Luke places it on the Mount of Olives just outside Jerusalem (Matthew 28:16-20; Luke 24:45-53).

There is one more Resurrection appearance in the Gospels, occurring only in John's Gospel, and it is this one I'd like to focus on, for it brings things full circle for Peter.

Breakfast by the Lake

To appreciate the significance of this story, we need to return to where our story began. It was early in the morning. Simon and Andrew, James and John, and their hired men were cleaning the nets. They fished all night long, but had nothing to show for it. Jesus was walking along the lakeshore teaching the people. He stepped into Simon's boat and asked him to push the boat away from the shore so he could teach without being trampled by the crowd. Following his message, Jesus told Simon to go out into the deeper waters and cast out his net. When Simon did as Jesus said, he caught an amazing haul of fish—so many he needed help pulling them all in.

Three years later, we find what is, in John's Gospel, Jesus' last conversation with Peter before he leaves the disciples. The parallels between Luke's account of Simon's calling and John's account of the reinstatement of Simon cannot be missed.

In John's post-Easter account (as with Matthew), some time after the first appearances of Jesus, the disciples returned to Galilee. Seven of them are together on this particular occasion: Simon Peter, Thomas, Nathanael, James, John, and two other unnamed disciples. It is told as a personal reminiscence from John. It's after supper and Simon Peter says to the others, "I'm going fishing." The others respond, "We'll go with you." They set out in their boat, fished all night, and, as on the day Jesus called them three years earlier, they caught nothing.

It was early the next morning, and they were one hundred yards from shore when they saw a man standing around a fire, cooking fish for breakfast. He shouted out to them, "So, did you catch anything?" I've asked that question many times when seeing people fishing. The stranger on the shore knew the answer before he asked the question. "No!" they shouted in response. The man shouted back, "Cast your net on the right side of the boat and you will find some" (John 21:6).

As they lowered their nets, suddenly their nets were filled with fish, so many they couldn't haul in the net. It was John (assuming he was the "beloved disciple") that instantly knew who the man was on shore. The man on the shore was the same one who had told Simon Peter to cast out the nets into the deep water three years earlier, a catch of fish that changed their lives forever. "It's the Lord!" John says to Simon, who had yet to put two and two together.

Simon grabbed his cloak (fishermen routinely fished in their loincloth), put it on and jumped into the water, running as fast as he could in the relatively shallow waters along the coastline, unwilling to wait for the boat to get back to shore. I love the passion and affection expressed in this small detail of the story.

When the others arrived at the shore, they found Jesus roasting fish and preparing bread over the fire, as people still do today along the shore at the Sea of Galilee. How many times had they shared a meal of fish and loaves with him over the last three years? And how could they forget, as the nets were still sitting in the water, of the times he'd multiplied the fish and the loaves?

Jesus said to Simon, "Bring some of the fish that you've just caught" (v. 10). Simon went and drew the net to shore. The word "drew" (v. 11 KJV) here is, in Greek, the same word John uses when Jesus spoke of drawing people to him in John 12:32: "When I am lifted up from the earth, I will draw everyone to me." John writes his Gospel in layers. There is the surface level at which the reader takes things at face value. But there is always another layer, in which John wishes us to see a deeper meaning. This is why the early church called John the "spiritual gospel." Was Peter's pulling in the huge haul of fish meant to be a picture John wanted to paint of Peter's role in the early church, one who

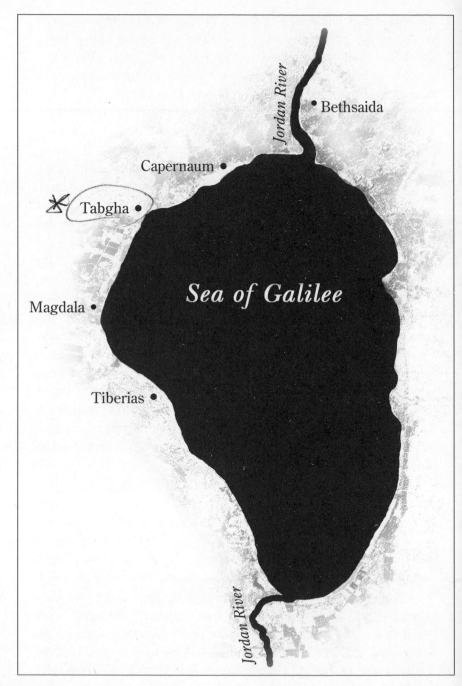

These heart-shaped stones, once columns in an ancient building, are strewn on the beach at Tabgha next to the church that marks the place where Jesus reinstated Peter by the Sea of Galilee. The heart is meant to represent Jesus' question, "Peter do you love me?"

would lead the church drawing others to Christ? Was it John's way of recounting that Jesus called Simon and the others to be "fishers of people"?

John tells us that when they counted the fish, there were 153 fish in the net. Often when John gives this level of detail the detail is symbolic. Yet no one in either the early church or today has been clear about the meaning of this number. Absent clear evidence as to its meaning, we can at least say that this was a large haul of large fish, and it likely pointed to the vast numbers of people of all nations that would come to faith in part because of Peter's ministry.

Christians today remember this story at a place called Tabgha. It's on the Sea of Galilee just about a mile and a half southwest of Capernaum. The name *Tabgha* means "seven springs," for the number of springs at the site that send fresh water flowing into the Sea of Galilee. The first church was built here in the AD 300s, marking one of the places where Jesus multiplied the fish and the loaves to feed the multitudes (the other being near Bethsaida). In the 1800s a group of German Catholics was preparing to build a hostel there, and they unearthed a tile mosaic from an ancient church depicting fish and bread. A chapel was erected over this site, just off the shoreline. It is also here at the shoreline that Christians remember the story of Jesus' appearance to his disciples, and his conversation with Peter, following the resurrection.

Peter, Do You Love Me?

There are several important details in this story of the meal on the seashore with Peter, Jesus, and the others. Once again, Jesus is breaking bread with his disciples. In John's Gospel, the breaking of bread is usually pointing towards the Eucharist. So it is a kind of Communion with the Lord that takes place on the shore. This Communion is also what we see in Luke's account of the two disciples on the road to Emmaus. You may recall that the two didn't realize that the stranger walking with them was Jesus until he joined them for supper. Only after he broke bread and blessed it were their eyes opened and they recognize Jesus.

In John's story at the lakeshore, Jesus invites his disciples to eat with him. The English word *companion* comes from a Latin word meaning "to break bread with." A companion is one with whom we share bread. Jesus chose a meal as the way in which his followers would continue to remember and commune with him. On this occasion, Jesus would once more invite his disciples to break bread with him— this becomes a eucharistic meal.

We speak of Holy Communion as "the Lord's Supper." The invitation to Holy Communion from the traditional liturgies noted, "Christ our Lord invites to his table all who do truly and earnestly repent of their sins...." The Eucharist, Lord's Supper, Holy Communion, whatever you call this meal, is a meal aimed not only at remembering and connecting us with Christ and one another as his disciples, it is also a meal of reconciliation and forgiveness. This meal at the shoreline was all of these things for Simon Peter.

It was at the Last Supper that Jesus predicted the disciples would fall away from him. And it was at that same supper that Peter said, "Even if I must die alongside you, I won't deny you" (Matthew 26:35). This meal at the shoreline would be a reconciliation set against the backdrop of the falling away that happened at the Last Supper. In the same way, every time *we* receive the Eucharist it is an opportunity for reconciliation.

John, always ready to give hints as to the deeper meaning of the story, tells us that Jesus was cooking over a *charcoal* fire. Some English translations make this clear, others simply call it a fire. But the Greek word is quite specific, *anthrakian*. The word only occurs in one other place in the Gospels, in John 18:18 where Simon Peter is warming himself at a *charcoal* fire outside the high priest's house, while Jesus is on trial inside. It was at this fire that Simon Peter would deny knowing Jesus three times. Now, at another charcoal fire, Jesus would thrice ask Simon, "Do you love me?"

In preparing this meal for his disciples, Jesus has once more taken the role of a servant, or a gracious host. Previously, he washed his disciples feet. Now, he prepares a meal for them.

It is interesting to note that here, as in most of the Resurrection appearances, there was some question as to whether the one they were seeing was, in fact, Jesus. At first, Mary Magdalene thought that Jesus was the gardener when she saw him. It was only after Jesus spoke Mary Magdalene's name that she recognized him. The two disciples on the road to Emmaus only saw a stranger until Jesus gave thanks, blessed and broke the bread for their evening meal. In Matthew, as Jesus stood before the disciples giving Great Commission, "some doubted." Thomas needed to see Jesus' wounds before he would believe. And here, John writes, "None of the disciples could bring themselves to ask him, 'Who are you?' They knew it was the Lord" (John 21:12). I wonder, did Jesus appear different in his resurrected state? Did he intentionally leave some ambiguity? Was Jesus requiring some measure of faith to see it was him? It wasn't by his outward appearance that they knew it was Jesus, but by his mannerisms, his voice, by what he said or did.

After the meal, Jesus turned to Peter and asked him, "Simon son of John, do you love me more than these?" (v. 15). What specifically was Jesus asking here? Was he asking, as some scholars suggest, "Simon, do you love me more than you love your friends and your life as a fisherman?" Reading the text this way, Jesus is saying, "If you really love me more than your friends and your old life, then feed my lambs." The metaphor for Peter's call moves from "fisher of people" to "shepherd of the flock." He's once more asking Simon to leave his old life and to continue and expand the mission to which Jesus had called him.

A second way to read this question, and the one I find more compelling, is to hear the question in the light of the Last Supper, particularly as Matthew describes it.* At the Last Supper as Matthew recounted it, Simon had implied that he loved Jesus more than the other disciples: "Even if I must die alongside you, I won't deny you" (26:35). But by now they all knew how Simon had in fact denied knowing Jesus on that fateful night. So the uncomfortable question Jesus was asking was, "Simon, do you *really* love me more than these [other disciples do]?" It was as if Jesus was subtly reminding Simon of that night when he pledged that, though the others might fall away, he would not.

This time, Peter didn't suggest that he loved Jesus more than the other disciples, but he did say, "Yes, Lord, you know I love you." Jesus said to him, "Feed my lambs." The fisher of men is now to be the pastor to the flock, a role that Jesus had announced for himself in John 10:11, "I am the good shepherd." Now he's asking Peter to carry on this role.

Regardless of which interpretation we take, the point is the same in the end. Jesus is questioning Simon's allegiance, commitment, and love. It's a line of questioning that would have been uncomfortable one-on-one, but was even more so because it took place in front of the other disciples. For each of the three denials, Jesus asks Simon if he indeed loves Jesus. And

---

* One could argue that John didn't know of Matthew's account of the Last Supper since he doesn't include it in his Gospel, but there are many things that John seems to know about that he chooses not to include, yet strongly hints at, including the Eucharist itself.

how would Simon prove his love for Jesus? By feeding Christ's sheep, or caring for his lambs.

Some interpreters make much of the fact that, in the Greek of John's Gospel, Jesus has asked, "Simon, do you love me?" using the Greek word, *agapao*, while Simon responds with, "You know I love you," using the Greek word, *phileo.* Agapao and *phileo* were at times used interchangeably in Greek. At others times there is a nuance to their meaning. I leave it to you, the reader, to research and decide what you think. What is most important and clear in the text is that Jesus was asking Simon to examine himself and to reaffirm his love three times, in light of the three denials Simon made at Caiaphas's house.

This was a psychological and spiritual examination, a means of penance and reconciliation. It forced Simon Peter to deal with his denial of Jesus, something that does not appear to have happened up to this point in any of the Gospel accounts of Jesus' appearance to the disciples. By asking these questions, Jesus is both confronting Simon and reaffirming his call upon Simon to lead the church. The questions filled Simon with sadness, which is appropriate for repentance and reconciliation.

At the times when I am consciously aware that I have denied the Lord by my actions, it is easy to offer a quick prayer asking for forgiveness, and to assume the Lord has forgiven me and to go on. I recently had a parishioner who confessed their sin, and quickly said, "But I know that Jesus has already forgiven me." I wanted to say, "Slow down a bit. Yes, he's ever ready to forgive, but maybe it's important to spend a little time thinking about what happened and how you got to where you are, and how you ensure this doesn't happen again." When we move too quickly to forgiveness, we get what Dietrich Bonhoeffer referred to as "cheap grace." There is power in the process of confession and penance leading to authentic reconciliation.

Three times Simon denied Jesus. Three times Jesus asked for his love and loyalty, feeling Simon squirm a bit while wrestling with his denial. And three times Jesus reaffirmed his call for Simon to be the Rock upon which he would build his church.

123

Failure humbles us. But it also teaches us. Jesus was using Peter's failure to teach him. He humbled him to make sure that Peter understood what happened. I don't know anyone who enjoys failing. I don't know anyone who says, "I hope I can fail today." But failure is a great teacher. One of the greatest things it teaches us is humility. Some people—and there have been times when I was among them—have to experience failure in order to learn how to be the people God wants them to be.

All of us fail sometimes. And yet it may very well be that the best parts of our lives come after we fail, provided we learn the right lessons from our teacher. Simon Peter could have responded to Jesus by saying, "Lord, look at these other guys— they all fled. At least I followed you to Caiaphas's house. What do you have to say about them?" But Peter didn't do that. He accepted what Jesus was teaching him. In humility, he was learning from his failure and opening himself to what might come next. He was ready to be reinstated as the leader of the movement of Jesus' followers.

Oh, How I Love Jesus

You've heard the phrase that sometimes we "can't see the forest for the trees"? Or the idiom, "It is as plain as the nose on your face"? I find when it comes to this interchange between Jesus and Simon, interpreters, preachers, and ordinary Christians are often so focused on the reinstatement of Peter, or trying to discover if there is some important meaning to the fact that there are different Greek words used for *love*, *sheep*, and *know* in the passage, that we miss what might be the most important idea in this conversation.

There's a song I learned when I was in high school, whose chorus we would sing again and again. It goes like this, "O, how I love Jesus, O, how I love Jesus, O, how I love Jesus, because he first loved me!" It is easy to sing of our love for Jesus. But in this exchange between Jesus and Simon, Jesus says, "If you love me, then care for my sheep." Jesus' love for us was demonstrated by his death on the cross. Our love for him is demonstrated by our care for others. This is what Jesus was teaching in John 15:8 when he said, "My Father is glorified when you produce much fruit and in this way prove that you are my disciples." And what was the fruit he was looking for? He tells us in verse 12, "Love each other just as I have loved you." This is what John writes in 1 John 4:20, "The person who doesn't love a brother or sister who can be seen can't love God, who can't be seen."

The way we express our love for Jesus is by caring for others. This might literally involve feeding them, as Jesus taught in the parable of the sheep and the goats: "I was hungry, and you gave me something to eat." It might involve meeting others' need for clothing or shelter. It might involve caring for them when they are sick or visiting someone in prison. What we do for others, Jesus says, is an expression of our love and devotion to him. In his interchange with Peter, Jesus boiled it down to a simple command: if you love me, then feed my sheep, and care for my lambs.

We can pray and sing, "I love you Lord" and "O, how I love Jesus" until we're blue in the face, but the love Jesus was asking Simon for, was a love that was reflected in caring for others.

Dan and Emma lost their nineteen-year-old son, Hunter, this last year. They are two of the dearest and most remarkable people I know. Dan's impact on the Church of the Resurrection is incalculable—he has served on staff for twenty-seven years as of the writing of this book. Hunter's death moved the entire congregation. A couple of weeks after the funeral service, I was checking in on them, to see how they were holding up, and Emma described how God was bearing them through this pain. She said, "Adam, we have felt God in profound ways in every person who walked in the door of our home. People dropped off toilet paper or cookies or entire meals. They came and wanted to mow our yard. They mucked out the stalls in our barn and fed the horses. And some just came and wrapped their arms around us. Some of them were people we hardly even knew. In every one of them we felt God's presence." Each of these who cared for Dan and Emma and their family was responding to Jesus' call: "Do you love me? Feed my lambs." We are each, at times, the sheep in need of care, just as we are, at other times, called to be Simon Peter for others, called to feed the sheep and care for the lambs.

Jesus asks each of us, "Do you really love me? Then care for my lambs."

Lord, I have failed you many times. Forgive me. Wash me and make me new. I do love you. Help me to love you more. Use my hands. Use my lips. Use my time and my energy. Use all of me to feed your sheep. Make the person you want me to be. In your holy name. Amen.

6

THE REST
OF THE STORY

*[Jesus said to them,] "You will receive power when
the Holy Spirit has come upon you, and you will
be my witnesses in Jerusalem, in all Judea and
Samaria, and to the end of the earth."*

(Acts 1:8)

*When Pentecost Day arrived, they were all together
in one place. Suddenly a sound from heaven like
the howling of a fierce wind filled the entire house
where they were sitting. They saw what seemed to
be individual flames of fire alighting on each one
of them. They were all filled with the Holy Spirit
and began to speak in other languages as the Spirit
enabled them to speak.*

(Acts 2:1-4)

127

Peter... raised his voice and declared...

"Change your hearts and lives. Each of you must be baptized in the name of Jesus Christ for the forgiveness of your sins. Then you will receive the gift of the Holy Spirit. This promise is for you, your children, and for all who are far away—as many as the Lord our God invites." With many other words he testified to them and encouraged them, saying, "Be saved from this perverse generation." Those who accepted Peter's message were baptized. God brought about three thousand people into the community on that day.

(Acts 2:14, 38-41)

We've focused most of this book on Peter's life as found in the Gospels. We've seen Peter's courage and cowardice, his faithfulness and his failures. But following Jesus' resurrection, everything we know about Simon Peter is going to change, because he himself was about to change.

While we spent five chapters pondering some of the events of Simon's life in conjunction with the ministry of Jesus—covering just three years of Peter's life—in this final chapter we will turn to the Acts of the Apostles, and a bit of what we find in Paul's letters and the letters attributed to Peter, to catch a glimpse of the ministry of Simon Peter in the three decades following the death and resurrection of Jesus.

Waiting in the Upper Room

In the opening of the Acts of the Apostles, Luke records Jesus' final words to his disciples: "You will receive power when the Holy Spirit has come upon you, and you will be my witnesses in Jerusalem, in all Judea and Samaria, and to the end of the earth" (Acts 1:8). Jesus had previously promised to send

God's Spirit to comfort, guide, and lead his disciples after his death. The Spirit (the Greek word is *pneuma,* which may also be translated as wind or breath) is mentioned throughout the Old Testament. Often referred to as the LORD's spirit, or Yahweh's spirit, God's Spirit came upon individuals imbuing them with prophetic or artistic gifts, supernatural strength, wisdom, and understanding, and empowering them to speak in God's name. It was this same Spirit that Jesus was promising to his followers. They were to wait in Jerusalem for the coming of this Holy Spirit.

And so they waited. By the Jewish Feast of Pentecost, there were 120 people, men and women, who were waiting as Jesus requested, in prayer, in an upstairs guest room. This was likely the same gathering place where the disciples had shared the Last Supper, and where they had remained in hiding following the arrest and crucifixion of Jesus. The Twelve (Matthias had been chosen by this time to replace Judas) waited, but Luke tells us they were joined by the women who had been following Jesus, by Mary, the mother of Jesus, and by Jesus' brothers.*

If you were to visit Jerusalem searching for the upper room, you would likely be taken to a room called the Cenacle (from the Latin word for dining room). It is located over the place said to be King David's tomb. The room you would visit was built in the 1300s and is not the actual upper room, but the room Jesus and his disciples gathered in may have been located at the site. Often the Cenacle will be filled with tour groups from a wide array of countries. The low vaulted ceilings and hard surfaces make it a great place to sing. I was once in the room as groups from Korea, somewhere in Latin America, Africa, and the United States were all singing at the same time. It was a beautiful picture of what

---

* In the Catholic, Orthodox, and even among some Protestant traditions, where Mary is believed to have remained a virgin, never consummating her marriage to Joseph, these brothers are considered sons of Joseph by his deceased first wife, or cousins. Methodists will find it interesting that John Wesley affirmed this belief. See his 1749, "Letter to a Roman Catholic," section 7.

Top: An interior view of the Cenacle, one of the sites associated with the upper room where Jesus and the disciples ate the Last Supper.

Left: St. Mark's Syriac Orthodox Church and Convent claims to be at site of the house of St. Mary, mother of John Mark, which some believe was the location of the upper room.

happened on that first Pentecost as all 120 disciples were filled with the Spirit and spoke in languages that were not their own.

On my last visit to the Holy Land, I was encouraged to visit St. Mark's Syriac Orthodox Church and Convent by one of its members. It claims to be the actual site of the house of St. Mary, the mother of John Mark, and therefore, they believe, their church and convent are located at the precise location of the upper room. This is based upon Acts 12:12 where we read that Peter, freed from prison, "made his way to Mary's house. (Mary was John's mother; he was also known as Mark.) Many believers had gathered there and were praying." The library there contains many ancient church manuscripts, some dating to the fourth century. As with so many sites in the Holy Land, it would be impossible to tell if this were the location of the actual home of Mary. Nevertheless, it was a wonderful place to remember the story of what happened to and through Peter that empowered him to actually live into his name—to become the Rock upon which the church would be built.

Pentecost

Fifty days had now passed since the Passover when Jesus had transformed the seder meal into a meal to remember his death and the new covenant sealed by his blood. Passover commemorates the night God delivered the Israelites from slavery in Egypt. Fifty days after the Feast of Passover, the Jewish people celebrate Shavuot commemorating the giving of the Ten Commandments to Moses on Mount Sinai. *Shavuot* literally means "weeks" in Hebrew—it occurs seven weeks after Passover—and it is also the time when the early summer harvest was celebrated and when the first fruits of the harvest were brought as an offering to God. The name *Pentecost* is Greek, and it means fifty days.

Here's what Luke tells us happened on this day when Jews from around the world had gathered in Jerusalem to commemorate the giving of the Law and the harvest:

131

When Pentecost Day arrived, they were all together in one place. Suddenly a sound from heaven like the howling of a fierce wind filled the entire house where they were sitting. They saw what seemed to be individual flames of fire alighting on each one of them. They were all filled with the Holy Spirit and began to speak in other languages as the Spirit enabled them to speak.

(Acts 2:1-4)

These believers, including the disciples who had remained in hiding in this room fifty days earlier, spilled out into the streets. They could not help themselves. So filled with the Spirit and power of God, like the prophets of old, they began proclaiming the good news of God, only these did so in languages they had not known before, in the languages of the foreign Jews in the city for the festival.

Soon a huge crowd gathered. Some mocked this display, claiming the followers of Jesus were drunk. Then Peter, who not long before had been fearful of arrest, spoke up and gave the first sermon of the newborn church. It is found in Acts 2. I encourage you to read his entire message as Luke records it. Here, I'd like to share just the conclusion of the sermon and the response of the crowd:

"Let all Israel know beyond question that God has made this Jesus, whom you crucified, both Lord and Christ."

When the crowd heard this, they were deeply troubled. They said to Peter and the other apostles, "Brothers, what should we do?"

Peter replied, "Change your hearts and lives. Each of you must be baptized in the name of Jesus Christ for the forgiveness of your sins. Then you will receive the gift of the Holy Spirit. This promise is for you, your children,

and for all who are far away—as many as the Lord
our God invites." With many other words he testified
to them and encouraged them, saying, "Be saved from
this perverse generation." Those who accepted Peter's
message were baptized. God brought about three
thousand people into the community on that day.

(Acts 2:36-41)

Despite the risk that he would be arrested and possibly put to death, Peter proclaimed that Jesus was both Lord and Christ. He was the long-awaited Messiah (Christ) and he (not Caesar) was the rightful Ruler, not only of Israel, but of all people. Peter called the listeners to repentance, to recognize the ways in which they had turned from God's path, to yield their hearts and lives to God, asking for forgiveness and pledging to follow Christ.

And on that day, three thousand people said yes and became a part of Jesus' *ekklesia*—the church.

Each day I pray anew for the Holy Spirit to fill me. As I'm writing my sermons, I pray for the Spirit to speak to me and through me. I seek to pay attention to the Spirit's whispers and nudges, particularly as it relates to people who might need encouragement or care. When I do this, I find myself in the midst of meaningful ministry. I feel greater boldness. I see things I would not have otherwise seen. Each day as I've been writing this book, I have prayed for the Holy Spirit to use me to speak to you, the reader.

Recently, my old microwave oven died, and my friend Reed came over to help me put in a new one. The new one didn't quite fit in the built-in cabinet, so we were going to build a frame for the microwave to sit on. Reed, who is great at this kind of stuff, brought over a two-by-four for the frame and his power saw to cut it to size. He was using an 18-volt battery-operated circular saw. We measured, marked the wood where it needed to be cut, and set it up on a makeshift saw horse. Reed grabbed his circular saw, inserted a battery, set the saw at the place he was going to make his first cut, and pulled the trigger. Nothing happened. The battery was dead. "Don't worry," he said. "I have another battery." So he replaced the battery, tried again, and still nothing happened. He went through four batteries—they had been sitting in his garage so long, unused and out of their charging cradles, they were all dead. The saw had the potential to do the job that was needed easily, yet without charged batteries it was nothing more than an expensive paperweight.

This is how I think many of us live the Christian life. We fail to invite the Holy Spirit to empower us. We don't pursue the spiritual disciplines of prayer, worship, Scripture reading, silence, and others that open us to the Spirit's power. We are living Spirit-anemic Christian lives. Even preachers at times forget to avail themselves of the Spirit's power. I know because I've preached and led in seasons of my ministry when I was not attentive to or seeking the Spirit's power. Without the Spirit's work, we lead powerless, impotent, and sometimes even cowardly Christian lives. But with the Spirit we have power, beyond anything we could imagine, to spread the gospel, help make new disciples, and transform the world for Christ.

We are meant to live Spirit-filled, Spirit-led, Spirit-empowered lives. But God's Spirit will not typically work where there is not first an invitation.

Christ's resurrection clearly changed Peter's understanding of who Christ was, and the kind of Kingdom he was ushering in. But it was the power of the Holy Spirit given at Pentecost that enabled Peter to become the rock Jesus foretold that he would be.

Miraculous Healing, Holy Boldness

From Pentecost on, with the Spirit working through him, Peter was used by God to do amazing things—acts he had never done before, things he had only seen Jesus do. In the rest of this chapter I'd like to recount some of the amazing, bold, and courageous things God did through Peter as recorded in the Acts of the Apostles.

In Acts 3, Peter and John were going to the temple for the afternoon hour of prayer. As they prepared to enter, a man crippled since birth was sitting at the gate, asking for money. As he began to ask them for a gift, Peter spoke up,

> *"Look at us!" So the man gazed at them, expecting to receive something from them. Peter said, "I don't have any money, but I will give you what I do have. In the name of Jesus Christ the Nazarene, rise up and walk!" Then he grasped the man's right hand and raised him up. At once his feet and ankles became strong. Jumping up, he began to walk around. He entered the temple with them, walking, leaping, and praising God.*
>
> *(Acts 3:4b-8)*

Among all the lines in this story, it's the description of how the man went "walking, leaping, and praising God" that I love the most. In one sense, we're all a bit "crippled since birth." We're spiritually broken, crippled, lame. But in knowing Jesus Christ we find healing, hope, the ability to walk and leap and praise God. We become whole again in the light of God's work in us.

In the temple courts a crowd soon gathered to see this man, who had spent years begging at the temple. They marveled that he now leapt and danced. There, at the portion of the temple courts known as Solomon's Porch, Peter began to preach to this curious crowd a bold and courageous sermon. You can read it in Acts 3:12-26, the second recorded sermon of the early church. He had been afraid of the religious leaders just weeks before, but now stood in broad daylight at the temple courts, in full view of the religious leaders, proclaiming that the man they had crucified was risen, that Jesus was the Messiah, and that it was Jesus' name and power that had healed this man.

I've walked on the Temple Mount many times. One thing I would not do is try to preach there. I know that I would be quickly escorted off by the guards that watch over that place. Christians and Jews are not allowed to enter the area of the Al Aqsa Mosque and the Dome of the Rock carrying a prayer book or a Bible, or even an iPad that could be used as a prayer book. Security stands ready to make such persons leave. Yet it was much more dangerous for Simon Peter to preach in the temple courts as he does in Acts. Nevertheless, Simon Peter stood there preaching and calling the people to repentance and to follow Jesus as the long-awaited Christ. Here's what happened next:

> *While Peter and John were speaking to the people, the priests, the captain of the temple guard, and the Sadducees confronted them. They were incensed that the apostles were teaching the people and announcing that the resurrection of the dead was happening because of Jesus. They seized Peter and John and put them in prison until the next day.*
>
> *(Acts 4:1-3)*

The next day, Peter and John stood before the very council that condemned Jesus to death, and this time, Peter did not deny being Jesus' disciple. He boldly proclaimed that the man had been healed,

> *"because of the name of Jesus Christ the Nazarene— whom you crucified but whom God raised from the dead. This Jesus is the stone you builders rejected; he has become the cornerstone! Salvation can be found in no one else. Throughout the whole world, no other name has been given among humans through which we must be saved."*
>
> *(Acts 4:10b-12)*

The religious leaders were surprised by the two men's confidence and boldness, particularly as the council thought the two men were uneducated and not trained to stand before a court like this one. The council demanded that they stop speaking and teaching in the name of Jesus. Peter and John replied, "It's up to you to determine whether it's right before God to obey you rather than God. As for us, we can't stop speaking about what we have seen and heard" (Acts 4:19-20). Do you see the impact of the Holy Spirit on these disciples?

Have you ever felt that something was so remarkably good that you just had to share it with others? If you're a grandparent, or have friends who are grandparents, you've probably been on the giving or receiving end of this phenomenon. You want to show people photos of your grandkids. Recently as I was boarding a plane, I found myself doing just this with a complete stranger. I love my granddaughter so much I just can't help telling others about her. The excitement spills out of you. You can't keep it to yourself.

That's how Peter and the apostles felt about Jesus' impact on their lives. It was so profound that Peter had to share it. He couldn't stop talking about it. Has your faith impacted you in this way? Has your experience with the risen Christ been so life-giving that you had to share it? Have you been so filled by the Spirit that you just had to tell others about your faith in Christ?

A survey was conducted a couple of years ago of people who don't attend church. One of the questions was, "If someone you respected invited you to church, would you consider going?" Would it surprise you to learn that 60 percent said yes?

Can I ask you a question? How bold and courageous are you when it comes to letting others know that you are a disciple of Jesus? Admittedly there are many bad examples of Christians witnessing to their faith in ways that are off-putting. And there are some vocal Christians who may believe things quite different from you, or who act in ways you feel are hypocritical or judgmental. This is what I often hear from people who are hesitant to talk about their faith. But if Christians like you don't speak up, then the only Christians they will know are those that they find off-putting.

One of our church members was being highlighted for some remarkable humanitarian work that she had done. I so appreciated that in an interview she made a point to say, "I do this in part because I am trying to follow Jesus and these are the kinds of things he called his followers to do." Another member is a radio broadcaster. He has a way of mentioning his faith from time to time on his program. He's not preachy; it's just an important part of his life. We have professors, school teachers, and a wide array of others, and it has been exciting to watch them seeking to share their faith with humility and respect.

I've always appreciated the quote, often attributed to St. Francis of Assisi though I am uncertain if he actually said it, that goes, "Preach the gospel at all times. Use words when necessary." I find many Christians are pretty good at preaching the gospel by actions, which is really important. Where we get a bit more nervous is actually using the words. But sometimes, you've got to be able to speak about the love of God, who came to us in Jesus. We must be able to describe our experience of his love and mercy. We believe that Jesus is the source of hope and light and life.

Do you live in such a way that the people around you know that you are a Christian? Do people know that you go to church? Is your faith one that would lead them to want to know more? I'd encourage you to come up with an "elevator speech"—a brief description of your faith and how it makes a difference in your life. Are there ways in social media posts that you can share your faith with others? Both good deeds and the ability to describe your faith to others are important. At least that's what Peter wrote in 1 Peter 3:15-16: "Whenever anyone asks you to speak of your hope, be ready to defend it. Yet do this with respectful humility, maintaining a good conscience."

By Acts 5, the Christian faith was spreading in remarkable ways. Peter was not just a rock, but something of a "rock star." Listen to what Acts 5:14-16 notes:

Indeed, more and more believers in the Lord, large numbers of both men and women, were added to the church. As a result, they would even bring the sick out into the main streets and lay them on cots and mats so that at least Peter's shadow could fall on some of them as he passed by. Even large numbers of persons from towns around Jerusalem would gather, bringing the sick and those harassed by unclean spirits. Everyone was healed.

Shortly after this, the apostles were once again arrested by the Jerusalem Council. Once more they commanded the disciples to stop preaching and teaching in the name of Jesus. Once more Peter spoke up and said, "We must obey God rather than humans!" (5:29). This was the Rock Jesus saw in the young fisherman! The Council had Peter and the others beaten this time. Yet they left the beating "rejoicing because they had been regarded as worthy to suffer disgrace for the sake of the name" (5:41).

Beyond Jerusalem

From Jerusalem, as Luke tells us, Peter first traveled to Samaria to support Phillip's work there (Acts 8:14-17). Later he traveled toward the Mediterranean coast, stopping in a town called Lydda, about twenty-five miles northwest of Jerusalem. There he encountered a man who had been paralyzed for eight years. When Peter prayed for him, suddenly the man was able to walk. That drew even more people to hear the gospel of Jesus.

While Peter was in Lydda, a much-loved believer named Tabitha (Dorcas in Greek) became deathly ill. She lived in Joppa, some ten miles away from Lydda. When she died, the

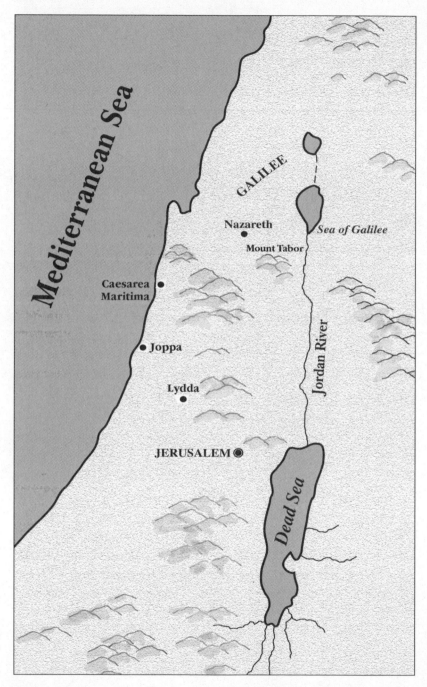

believers in Joppa did something strange. They sent for Simon Peter and asked him to come quickly to Joppa. Did they hope he would preach her funeral? Or minister to her family? Or did they actually think that Peter might pray for her and she'd live again?

Peter did go to Joppa (known as Jaffa today), at least a half-day's journey away. When he arrived, everyone was weeping. He was taken to an upper room, where Tabitha had been prepared for her burial. Peter sent everyone out of the room, knelt next to her, and prayed. Then he turned to Tabitha's dead body and said, "Tabitha, get up!" She opened her eyes and, seeing Peter, she sat up. He took her hand and helped her up.

This is the apex of the miracle stories of Peter that are recounted in Acts. Jesus had, on three occasions, raised the dead. Peter now participates in this same work. What is important to note is that these miraculous deeds of compassion and healing served to open the door to Peter's preaching the gospel. The deeds preceded the proclamation. Following Tabitha's resuscitation, "The news spread throughout Joppa, and many put their faith in the Lord" (Acts 9:42).

How I wish I could pray over the dying or recently dead and they would sit up. I've prayed for many who were ill and dying. I've knelt next to their hospital beds at times. I've even laid flat on the floor in my home—prostrate, as the Bible calls it—praying for some who were deathly ill. Occasionally, I've seen people made well, or their lives extended, in ways that defied medical explanation.

I was visiting with a woman last week at church who had experienced such a miracle. Twenty years ago, she had been diagnosed with cancer and the outlook was not good. She had three daughters in the home and a marriage that was struggling. To everyone's surprise, she recovered and is still here twenty years later. Was it her body's miraculous response to the oncologist's treatment? Was it the miraculous nature of the treatment? Or was it the power of God healing her directly? We can't know. What I do know is that for every one of these stories, there are many more of people who find hope and strength from their faith, even if they do not experience a miraculous healing.

We call stories like Peter's healing of Tabitha miracles because they are rare. They are not God's ordinary way of working in the world. God doesn't ordinarily suspend the biological and physiological laws by which our bodies operate solely because we've prayed and have faith. Because of this, it would be easy to conclude that miracles never happen. But the biblical stories, and my own experiences, lead me to think that, on occasion, for reasons I may never fully understand, God's Spirit and power bring about an unexpected result: a miracle. It often happens in concert with the medical treatment and our body's own built-in system for fighting off disease but sometimes in ways that even the medical doctors cannot explain.

Regardless of whether the miraculous answer to prayer occurs, when we demonstrate compassion and kindness to others in their hour of need, as when Peter traveled a half-day's journey to Joppa to pray with a dead woman's friends and family, people are impacted by our kindness. Even when Tabitha doesn't open her eyes, God's kingdom comes, even if it is through our comfort, compassion, and acts of selfless love.

"Take and Eat, Peter"

Peter remained in Joppa, staying, Acts tells us, in the home of Simon the Tanner. If you visit Joppa today, you'll find that Joppa, or Jaffa as it is known, is it a suburb of the larger city of Tel-Aviv. There are 438,000 people living in this coastal metropolis where the sun shines 320 days a year. It is a beautiful place to walk along the beach. Tel-Aviv is a new city; Joppa has been around for three thousand years. If you visit the old city of Joppa, you'll find art galleries and restaurants. And, down a small alley leading to a dead end, you'll find a wall and a door that claims to be where Simon the Tanner's house stood. A small Muslim minaret rises above the wall, and a Muslim place of prayer stands on the other side of the door. Muslims revere Simon Peter as a disciple of

This door stands at the site where Simon the Tanner's house is said to have stood. It is now a Muslim place of prayer, with a small minaret rising above the wall.

Jesus. For Muslims, Jesus is the greatest prophet aside from Muhammad and Jesus' disciples were steadfast believers. Peter is called Butrus in Islam, after the Arabic word for rock. Shia Muslims consider him the first imam to follow Jesus, and the prince of the apostles. Hence in the 1700s, a Muslim family built a small mosque and minaret here to honor his memory.

Acts 10 narrates a pivotal story for the Christian faith. It was noon, and Peter had gone up to pray on the rooftop of Simon the Tanner. He was hungry and ready to eat. Others were preparing the meal while he was praying. Simon went into something like a trance, and he saw a vision of something like a sheet being lowered by its four corners from heaven. Inside were animals that the Torah, the most authoritative part of Peter's Scriptures, clearly identified as unclean and not to be eaten. He knew these laws. As a fisherman, Peter had thrown back thousands of fish

143

in his life that had no scales (fish without scales were deemed unclean by the Torah). Among the animals the Torah deemed unclean and not to be eaten were camels, pigs, frogs, hawks, owls, snails, shrimp, and a variety of others. Yet in his vision, Peter heard a voice from heaven saying,

"Get up, Peter! Kill and eat!"

But Peter exclaimed, "Absolutely not, Lord! I have never eaten anything impure or unclean."

The voice spoke a second time, "Never consider unclean what God has made pure."

(Acts 10:13-15).

This vision and command are repeated *three times*. One can imagine how bewildering this was to Simon Peter. His Bible, in particular the Law of Moses, gave clear instructions about God's will regarding food. But now, in his vision, he has heard what seems to have been the voice of God, telling him to kill and eat what was specifically forbidden in the Torah. Had God changed his mind? Was Peter hearing the voice of the tempter? What does this mean?

Just then there was a knock on the door. Men from the port city of Caesarea Maritima, thirty miles to the north, had come looking for a Simon Peter. They were servants of a Roman centurion named Cornelius, who just the day before had a vision of an angel telling him to send messengers to Joppa to find a man named Peter, staying at Simon the Tanner's house, and to summon him.

As a centurion in the Italian company, Cornelius was a high-ranking and respected member of the Roman military. But Luke tells us he and his household were also, "pious, Gentile God-worshippers. He gave generously to those in need among the Jewish people and prayed to God constantly" (Acts 10:2). Cornelius did as the angel in his vision commanded. He sent two of his household servants and a member of his military staff.

It was these who were now knocking on Simon the Tanner's door. They explained about Cornelius's vision, and Peter put two and two together. His vision of the unclean food that God had declared clean was God's way of telling him that, despite what he had learned growing up about clean and unclean, Jew and Gentile, God was doing something new.

For Jews of this period, the non-Jew was not technically one's neighbor. The call to love your neighbor as you love yourself was interpreted to mean your fellow Jew. Instead, Gentiles were seen as a source of defilement. Associating more closely than the minimum required might lead to idolatry or some other form of sinfulnesss or compromise of one's faith. While the Torah did not, at least not that I can recall, suggest it was a sin to eat in the home of a Gentile, certain passages were interpreted this way in rabbinic Judaism and this was widely held to be the truth about God's will. But here these Gentiles were, knocking on Simon the Tanner's door.

Peter invited the men to spend the night, an unusual situation inviting non-Jews to stay in Simon the Tanner's home. The next day they left for Caesarea. Meanwhile, Cornelius gathered all of his close friends, anticipating Peter's arrival. When Peter arrived, he was welcomed by a large gathering of people, most of them presumably Gentiles. Once again, we hear Peter preaching the good news of Jesus Christ; I encourage you to read his message for yourself in Acts 10:34-43.

While Peter was speaking, Luke tells us, the Holy Spirit fell upon all who heard him. They, too, spoke in other languages as Peter and the 120 had done on the day of Pentecost. But these were uncircumcised *Gentiles*. Realizing that they had received the Spirit, even though they were not converts to Judaism and had not been circumcised, Peter asks, "These people have received the Holy Spirit just as we have. Surely no one can stop them from being baptized with water, can they?" He directed that they be baptized in the name of Jesus Christ. Then they invited Peter to stay for several days" (Acts 10:47-48).

145

And apparently Peter did stay in the home of this Gentile family, who were baptized as Christ followers yet not circumcised as Jews. It was quite confusing and unsettling. Peter made a judgment call not based upon an argument from Scripture, but based upon a vision he had experienced and seeing the Holy Spirit falling upon Cornelius and his friends.

This is a remarkable story. In Acts 10:34-35 Peter says, "I really am learning that God doesn't show partiality to one group of people over another. Rather, in every nation, whoever worships him and does what is right is acceptable to him." This is a profound statement; Peter was still learning. His old views were changing. What he thought he knew about God and God's grace was being turned on its head. Even how he read and interpreted Scripture was changing in response to seeing God working in the lives of those he previously considered unclean.

I wonder if you ever have been surprised by God's grace. Have you been surprised to see God working in the lives of people you may not have expected? I came to faith when I was fourteen in a little Pentecostal church, a part of the Assemblies of God denomination. They were a wonderful group of people. They welcomed me and loved me, and God used them to change my life. It was there I heard the call to full-time ministry.

On the denomination's logo back then, were the letters AG, for Assemblies of God, and a small open Bible that said, "All the Gospel." The acronym AG captured both the denominational name, and the idea that our church held to "all the gospel." Implicit in this, in my fourteen-year-old mind, was that my friends who went to other churches did not have "all the gospel." It was my take on things.

It was such a surprise to me, when I went to a Christian college and met professors and fellow students of other denominations, to discover others whose faith and knowledge of God was broader and deeper than mine. They had other ways of interpreting some of the same Scriptures that seemed just as sound as what I had learned. And as I looked at their lives, I saw a clear evidence of the Holy Spirit. It humbled me and changed my perspective.

In a day and time when people are increasingly polarized, both politically and ideologically, Peter's insight in Cornelius's home seem important to remember: "I really am learning that God doesn't show partiality to one group of people over another. Rather, in every nation, whoever worships him and does what is right is acceptable to him" (Acts 10:34-35).

But that insight was a bit unsettling to the other leaders of the church back in Jerusalem. Here's what Luke says happened when Peter returned: "The apostles and the brothers and sisters throughout Judea heard that even the Gentiles had welcomed God's word. When Peter went up to Jerusalem, the circumcised believers criticized him. They accused him, 'You went into the home of the uncircumcised and ate with them!'" (Acts 11:1-3).

It's interesting that these disciples were criticizing Simon Peter with the exact same criticism the Pharisees used to criticize Jesus and his disciples, "The Pharisees and their legal experts grumbled against his disciples. They said, 'Why do you eat and drink with tax collectors and sinners?'" (Luke 5:30). It's so easy and natural for us to see others as unclean and to separate ourselves from the other and stand in judgment of them. Humans have a long history of doing just this.

But, "step-by-step, Peter explained what had happened" and, as the believers in Jerusalem heard of Peter's vision and the Holy Spirit's work among the Gentiles, Luke notes, "they calmed down. They praised God and concluded, 'So then God has enabled Gentiles to change their hearts and lives so that they might have new life'" (Acts 11:5, 18).

Luke devotes two chapters to this story, and for good reason. This is the hinge point not only of the Book of Acts, but of the entire Christian faith. Had this vision and Cornelius's conversion not occurred, Christianity may have remained a small sect within Judaism. Instead, it fulfilled the promise God had made to Abraham, that "all the families of the earth will be blessed because of you" (Genesis 12:3b). Today nearly a third of the world's population claim to be followers of Jesus.[1]

Continuing Conflict in the Church

In Paul's letter to the Galatians, written around AD 50, he describes a time when he and Barnabas were leading the church in Antioch (the Antioch in what is today southeast Turkey). The church was made up largely of Gentiles. Peter had come to visit the church, to minister and give leadership to the believers there. He ate freely with Gentiles and shared full fellowship with them until some of the other Jewish Christians from Jerusalem arrived. Let's let Paul tell the story:

> *When Cephas [Peter] came to Antioch, I opposed him to his face, because he was wrong. He had been eating with the Gentiles before certain people came from James. But when they came, he began to back out and separate himself, because he was afraid of the people who promoted circumcision. And the rest of the Jews also joined him in this hypocrisy so that even Barnabas got carried away with them in their hypocrisy. But when I saw that they weren't acting consistently with the truth of the gospel, I said to Cephas in front of everyone, "If you, though you're a Jew, live like a Gentile and not like a Jew, how can you require the Gentiles to live like Jews?"*
>
> *(Galatians 2:11-14)*

The church would continue to wrestle with the question of whether Gentiles needed to become Jewish converts, be circumcised, and follow the Law in order to be part of the Christian community, or whether the only requirements were faith in Christ, repentance, and baptism. Paul would strongly advocate for the latter. And Peter found himself, at times, caught between these two sides.

The early church would spend decades wrestling with the question of the Gentiles, with strong opinions on both sides. On the one hand, most of the earliest followers of Jesus were Jewish. The Law was very important to them. It represented God's timeless word to his people. And when it came to circumcision, this command preceded the Law, being given to Abraham. It mattered so much to God that Moses was nearly put to death for not having circumcised his son (Exodus 4:24-26). These Jewish Christians had become, likely at great personal cost, followers of Jesus Christ. Some of them, like Paul, had been trained as Pharisees. They were serious about their faith in Jesus and in their desire to please God. They struggled to understand how Paul, of all people, could suggest that the Gentiles did not need to be circumcised or follow the Law of Moses. Christians were, after all, seeking to please God and to follow the Jewish Messiah.

Paul's case for setting aside the requirements of the Law and circumcision seemed to them to be built on a flimsy and entirely subjective rationale that served to diminish the authority of Scripture. It was unthinkable to them. We can see how strongly this sense of conviction was when we look at Peter's visceral reaction to the vision and the command to kill and eat the unclean animals, "Absolutely not, Lord!"

Paul offered a theological and biblical rationale for ending the requirements of circumcision and the Law, one that contemporary Christians still find a bit confusing, as any discussion of the continuing role of the Law in the believer's life will demonstrate. You can read it, as it was more fully fleshed out, in Paul's letter to the Romans. His arguments were convincing to him and others, but they seemed like so much rationalization to the Christians advocating continuing adherence to the Law and the requirement of circumcision.

For Peter, the idea that Gentiles did not need to be circumcised and fulfill the requirements of the Law seemed less about a fully developed theological position and more about

149

seeing the Holy Spirit at work in Cornelius and his family and other Gentile believers, as well as the vision he had of God declaring clean what the Scriptures had declared unclean (the unclean animals in his vision).

This was the first of many periods of intense debate within the history of Christianity over matters of theology, ethics, and the interpretation of Scripture. Today, the conflict in the church is over same-gender marriage and the continuing debate about what will be required of gay and lesbian people if they are to be fully a part of the Christian community. The church is asking, Are gay and lesbian Christians allowed to marry or must they remain celibate? For gay and lesbian people who are legally married and have families and who wish to be a part of the church, must they divorce and pledge celibacy in order to be fully a part of the congregation? There are a host of other questions circling around same-gender marriage and the church. Underneath this current debate, as with the first-century debate about circumcision, are questions about the interpretation of Scripture. And, as with the circumcision debate, there are committed followers of Jesus on both sides who at times struggle to see how the other side cannot see the truth as they see it.

The last time we hear from Peter in the Acts of the Apostles is in Acts 15, when Paul and Barnabas have come to Jerusalem for a definitive ruling from the leaders of the church there concerning the question of the Gentiles. Acts 15 begins,

> *Some people came down from Judea teaching the family of believers, "Unless you are circumcised according to the custom we've received from Moses, you can't be saved." Paul and Barnabas took sides against these Judeans and argued strongly against their position.*
>
> *The church at Antioch appointed Paul, Barnabas, and several others from Antioch to go up to Jerusalem to set this question before the apostles and the elders. . . .*

150

When they arrived in Jerusalem, the church, the apostles, and the elders all welcomed them. They gave a full report of what God had accomplished through their activity. Some believers from among the Pharisees stood up and claimed, "The Gentiles must be circumcised. They must be required to keep the Law from Moses."

The apostles and the elders gathered to consider this matter.

(Acts 15:1-2, 4-6)

Peter speaks up before the Council and takes the side of Paul, saying,

"Fellow believers, you know that, early on, God chose me from among you as the one through whom the Gentiles would hear the word of the gospel and come to believe. God, who knows people's deepest thoughts and desires, confirmed this by giving them the Holy Spirit, just as he did to us. He made no distinction between us and them, but purified their deepest thoughts and desires through faith. Why then are you now challenging God by placing a burden on the shoulders of these disciples that neither we nor our ancestors could bear? On the contrary, we believe that we and they are saved in the same way, by the grace of the Lord Jesus."

(Acts 15:7-11)

Paul and Barnabas went on to tell of what God had done among the Gentiles not only in Antioch, but on their first missionary journey in Asia Minor. Following this, the elders and apostles in Jerusalem made a declarative decision that was meant to settle the matter. The Gentiles would not be required to be circumcised, nor were they bound to follow the Law of Moses, but they were to "refuse food offered to idols, blood, the

151

meat from strangled animals, and sexual immorality" (15:29). This, of course, did not settle the matter. Christians continue to debate this question of the relationship of Christians to the Law and to circumcision to the present time. And Paul's own interpretation of the ruling of the Council led him to offer a different answer to the Christians at Corinth on the issue of food sacrificed to idols than the decision of the Council in Acts (see 1 Corinthians 8:1-13 and 10:25).

I love that in our last glimpse of Peter in Acts, he's actually working with Paul, in agreement that the grace of God extended to the Gentiles, without circumcision or obedience to the Law. It was grace that led to their inclusion in Christ's *ekklesia*. Despite some wavering in Antioch, here Peter speaks up clearly and decisively for Paul's position.

Frederick Faber penned a hymn in 1862, during a time of conflict among Christians in England that captured well Peter's insight that day in Cornelius' home, repeated before the Council of Jerusalem:

> There's a wideness in God's mercy like the wideness of the sea;
> there's a kindness in God's justice, which is more than liberty....
>
> For the love of God is broader than the measures of our mind;
> and the heart of the Eternal is most wonderfully kind.[2]

This meeting of the Jerusalem Council may be the last we hear of Peter in Acts, but Peter's words and influence paved the way for the Christian faith to spread, unabated, across the Roman Empire and around the world.

Peter's Final Years and His Death

While we can't be sure precisely when Peter came to Rome, or how often and for how long he was there, the early church was in universal agreement that he was there in the mid-60s while Nero was emperor of Rome.

Nero came to power in AD 54 and ruled until he took his own life in 68. He was not quite seventeen when he came to power. The Roman historian Suetonius, writing several decades after Nero's death in his *Lives of the Caesars*, paints a very dark portrait of Nero. The emperor's cruelty, debauchery, and depravity knew no ends. In addition, he had his mother and two of his wives killed, as well as other close family members. He squandered vast sums of money on building projects while often ignoring the plight of his people. And this is really just the tip of the iceberg of what was broken in this man.

Among the desires of Nero's heart was to refashion the city of Rome. But to do this would require clearing major sections of the city, something that would never have been possible— without a fire. On the evening of July 18, AD 64, a fire started in the city, sweeping through Rome with a terrible intensity. It burned throughout the day on July 19 and would continue for five more days before it was completely extinguished. Nero opened his home to the affected and personally assisted in the relief and recovery efforts, seeking to play the part of a heroic emperor. But there was widespread suspicion that he himself had orchestrated the fire for the express purpose of raising taxes and rebuilding the city according to his plans.

As people began to openly suggest that Nero was responsible, he sought to shift the blame to a community of people whose beliefs were already suspect: the Christians. Christians were held in suspicion in part because they had rejected Rome's old gods and, instead, followed a crucified Messiah. Nero made the Christians his scapegoat. The Roman historian Tacitus, who was born during Nero's reign, describes what happened to the Christians following the fire:

> Therefore, to scotch the rumour [that Nero had the city burned], Nero substituted as culprits, and punished with

Clockwise from left:

The Mamertine Prison in Rome, where Peter and Paul were imprisoned.

Prisoners at the Mamertine were lowered through a hole like this one, which was also used to give them food.

An interior view of one of the dungeons in the Mamertine.

the utmost refinements of cruelty, a class of men, loathed for their vices, whom the crowd styled Christians....They were covered with wild beasts' skins and torn to death by dogs; or they were fastened on crosses, and, when daylight failed were burned to serve as lamps by night. Nero had offered his Gardens for the spectacle, and gave an exhibition in his Circus, mixing with the crowd in the habit of a charioteer, or mounted on his car. Hence, in spite of a guilt which had earned the most exemplary punishment, there arose a sentiment of pity, due to the impression that they were being sacrificed not for the welfare of the state but to the ferocity of a single man.[3]

It seems likely that Peter was captured in this initial wave of persecution. Paul may have been arrested then, or within a year or two after this. Church tradition says that Peter, and later Paul, were held in the Mamertine Prison (also known as the Tullianum) just off the Roman Forum before their executions. The Church of San Giuseppe (Saint Joseph) is just above the prison.

If you visit the Mamertine in Rome, you'll be taken through a pretty impressive audiovisual presentation showing the history of the prison. It was in use as a prison long before Peter and Paul were kept there. Near the end of the tour, you will find yourself in a room with ancient frescoes on the walls and ceilings portraying Peter and Paul (these go back perhaps as early as the 600s). This room has been used as a chapel for Christian worship for at least 1,400 years. It was once an upper chamber of the jail. In the middle of the floor is a hole with a metal grate, what looks like a manhole cover. Prisoners would have been lowered or dropped through this hole, as was food or other necessities provided by family or friends of the imprisoned. Today the pit is accessed by a stairway that has been built to take visitors into the space. It is a stone room, dark, damp, about six feet high, and perhaps twenty by thirty feet across. In the past you could walk throughout the room. Recent renovations have created a metal walkway and railings that keep visitors from moving about freely in the room. In one portion of the floor there is an opening, like a basin, filled with water from an underground spring. One tradition has Peter (and another Paul) baptizing his fellow prisoners whom he led to Christ while in prison.

I've had the opportunity to have the room to myself, and had the lights turned off just to imagine it as it was when Peter spent his final days in this dungeon. The experience helped me visualize what Peter and Paul and any other prisoners in this pit would have experienced. As with nearly every holy site anywhere in the world, we cannot be sure that this was the exact location where Peter and Paul were imprisoned. Whether this was the prison or not, visiting the Mamertine has a way of helping those who enter to step into the stories of the final days of Christianity's leading apostles.

Imprisoned at separate times (one scholar places Peter's incarceration and death as October of AD 64[*] whereas Paul's was some time later), each of the apostles eventually was taken from this place to the place of their respective executions.[†] According to tradition, Paul was beheaded just outside the city walls. (Grisly as it seems now, beheading was regarded as a more merciful way to die, since it was quick and did not involve torture; it is likely that as a Roman citizen, Paul was spared one of Rome's more horrendous forms of execution.)

Peter met his death a different way. In John's Gospel, just after Jesus had thrice asked Peter if he loved him and challenged Peter to feed his sheep, he went on to tell Peter how he would meet his death:

---

[*] See Margherita Guarducci's in "The Date of Peter's Martyrdom," found at https://www.catholicculture.org/culture/library/view.cfm?recnum=5861.

[†] See my book, *The Call: The Life and Message of the Apostle Paul* (Nashville: Abingdon Press, 2015) for the story of the Apostle Paul including the traditions about his death in Rome.

*"I assure you that when you were younger you tied your
own belt and walked around wherever you wanted.
When you grow old, you will stretch out your hands
and another will tie your belt and lead you where you
don't want to go." He said this to show the kind of death
by which Peter would glorify God. After saying this,
Jesus said to Peter, "Follow me."*

(John 21:18-19)

The words "stretch out your hands" were used to describe
death by crucifixion, as the victims hands were stretched out
and affixed to the cross, often tied rather than nailed to the
cross. John wrote after Peter's death, and in this closing story in
his Gospel he seems to be hinting at the form of execution Peter
experienced.

According to the oldest traditions, Peter was taken to
Caligula's Circus, also known as Nero's Circus, the circus being
a large U-shaped track with stands where chariot races and
other large outdoor events were held. It was located in an area
of Rome called *Vaticanum*, the area which now is the Catholic
Church's headquarters and its own city-state. It is still known by
the name Vatican after its ancient designation. Here, Peter was
crucified.

The second-century apocryphal work, "The Acts of Peter,"
records an early tradition concerning Peter's crucifixion, in
which Peter says to those preparing to crucify him, "I beseech
you the executioners, crucify me thus, with the head downward
and not otherwise." The fourth-century "Acts of Peter and Paul"
expands the instruction with Peter's rationale,

Peter, having come to the cross, said: "Since my Lord
Jesus Christ, who came down from the heaven upon the
earth, was raised upon the cross upright, and He has
deigned to call to heaven me, who am of the earth, my
cross ought to be fixed head down, so as to direct my feet

St. Peter's Basilica is built at the site of Peter's tomb.

A view of the inside of St. Peter's Basilica, looking down from the dome.

158

towards heaven; for I am not worthy to be crucified like
my Lord." Then, having reversed the cross, they nailed
his feet up.[4]

While as a young man Simon Peter's faith at times faltered,
he now faced death with an indomitable faith. The First Epistle
of Peter may give us a clue as to how he faced his own death.
There Peter wrote, "Dear friends, don't be surprised about the
fiery trials that have come among you to test you. These are
not strange happenings. Instead, rejoice as you share Christ's
suffering. You share his suffering now so that you may also have
overwhelming joy when his glory is revealed" (4:12-13).[*]

Peter is believed to have been buried in a simple grave,
in what was a pagan graveyard near the place where he was
crucified, the Vatican Necropolis. Christians continued to visit
that place to honor Peter's memory. Beginning in the second
century, a street of beautifully adorned mausoleums was built
in this same place for some prominent families in Rome, again,
mostly pagan. In the fourth century, when Christianity was
legalized and eventually became the official state religion of
Rome, the first St. Peter's Basilica was built above Peter's tomb,
and the Necropolis was buried and the church built atop it.

The current St. Peter's Basilica was designed at different
times primarily by Michelangelo, Bernini, Bramante, and
Maderno, and was begun in 1506, and completed in 1626. If an
imaginary line ran straight down from the center of the dome
and continued underground, it would come to St. Peter's tomb.
In the 1940s, the Catholic Church undertook excavations under
the basilica to see if St. Peter's tomb could be identified—if it was,
in fact, even there. It was then that the amazing necropolis was
found, with much of the decorative artwork in the mausoleums
in amazing condition. It was years after the initial excavations
that a set of bones was identified, wrapped in purple and found

---

* There is some debate as to whether Peter wrote First Peter, and far more
  skepticism that Peter wrote Second Peter, but most in the early church accepted
  Peter's authorship of First Peter.

within a white marble box, believed by many to be the bones of St. Peter.

While in Rome, I had the opportunity to take the tour of the Vatican Necropolis beneath St. Peter's Basilica. It was fascinating. I was a skeptic that the Catholic Church had actually found the bones of St. Peter as I began the tour, but at the end, I found myself thinking that it was actually *possible* that these were in fact the bones of St. Peter. They were the bones of a man who was sixty to seventy years old, and about five feet six. Several books have been written on the archaeological work under the church, the necropolis, and the case for these being Peter's relics.

By the way, the archaeologists discovered that the center of the basilica's dome was in fact directly over the place where these bones had been found. Quite literally, the church was built on Peter the Rock.

Fishing for People

Simon Peter was a flawed yet ultimately a heroically faithful disciple. He was a fisherman, who heard the call of Jesus to join him in fishing for people. He was a shepherd, who fed and cared for the flock that was Christ's church. We're all flawed disciples, called to fish for people and care for Christ's sheep. And our hope should be that, when we get to the end of our lives, despite our failures, we will have been found faithful like Simon Peter.

I was sitting on the screened-in porch at the Lake of the Ozarks, working to finish this last chapter of the book, when I heard voices on the lake below. I walked out onto the deck and saw a small pontoon fishing boat just twenty feet off the shoreline. The back of the boat had ten or fifteen fishing poles and a woman who looked a bit tired of fishing. Her husband was at the wheel of the boat. And there in the front was a young man, maybe in his twenties. To my surprise, he was throwing out a casting net—the kind Peter and his friends would have used many times on the Sea of Galilee. In all my years coming to the lake, I'd never seen anyone use a casting net here. I'm sure they do, but I'd never seen it in our little cove or anywhere else.

I shouted out and asked the young man, "You catching anything with that?" He replied, "Just a few little ones." Then he added, "But you know how it is with fishing. You just gotta keep casting the net."

I had to laugh as I heard his words. It was somehow the perfect ending to months of reading and reflecting on Peter's life. Peter's calling began as he was coming in from a night of fishing. His awareness of the identity of Jesus came as he cast out the net and caught a miraculous haul of fish. Jesus called him to fish for people. He'd witnessed Jesus multiplying the fish and the loaves on two occasions. And following the Resurrection, it was another miraculous haul of fish that persuaded the apostles that the stranger on the shoreline really was Jesus. Peter would devote his life to fishing for people.

If you are a follower of Jesus, you've been called to fish for people—to help others see his love and grace through you. Like Peter, you'll fail sometimes, not just at fishing, but at following too. But Christ always takes you back and calls you to keep casting your net and fishing for people.

Lord, thank you for Peter's story. You know I've failed you many times. Thank you for always taking me back. Help me to be faithful to you. Help me to see the wideness to your mercy and to live my life in such a way that others are drawn to you through me. Equip me and use me to fish for people. Amen.

EPILOGUE: THE SILENT YEARS

In the final chapter, we jumped from Peter's speech at the Council in Jerusalem to his arrest and death in Rome in AD 64. Assuming the Council in Jerusalem was in the late 40's or perhaps as late as AD 50, what happened to Peter in the 15 or so years between the Council and his death in AD 64? These are often considered the "silent years" of Peter. Was he silent? That's not likely. If we've learned anything in this book, we've learned that silence is not Peter's strong suit. So, what can we say about this period?

We know that Peter began travelling through the Holy Land in ministry before the Jerusalem Council, which led him to Lydda, Joppa, and Caesarea. By the Jerusalem Council it is James, "the Lord's brother," who seems to be leading the Jerusalem Church, which tells us that Peter probably wasn't living in Jerusalem and or spending much time there. He had returned for the Council. It is likely that he had taken up Jesus' charge to take the gospel "to the uttermost parts of the earth" much as Paul had been doing.

Two epistles are attributed to Peter in the New Testament. We'll consider them in more detail in a moment. For now, I only want to note that First Peter is written "To God's chosen strangers in the world of the diaspora, who live in Pontus, Galatia, Cappadocia, Asia, and Bithynia" (1:1). These were all areas in what was called Asia Minor or Anatolia, modern-day Turkey. Paul had previously traveled in some of these areas starting churches. The fact that Peter is writing to these churches tell us that Peter himself had probably traveled throughout this area prior to writing the Epistle, visiting existing churches and possibly starting new ones.

Paul mentions Peter four times in his first letter to the Corinthians. It seems there were believers at Corinth who were claiming Peter as their apostle of choice. It is unlikely they would have had a strong affinity for Peter if they had never met him nor heard him speak. Hence it seems likely that Peter had preached somewhere on the Greek peninsula and that at least some in the church at Corinth had been moved by his ministry.

If you were a first-century Christian, how far would you be willing to travel, and to what lengths would you go, to meet someone who had spent three years with Jesus? Who actually lived the stories you had heard about? Who had seen the risen Lord? What impact would it have had on your faith? Would you have invited your friends to come and hear his stories? Paul had never met Jesus when he was alive; neither had Timothy or Titus or Apollos or most of the other traveling missionary preachers. Peter's missionary journeys would have played a tremendous role in confirming and strengthening the faith of the fledgling churches. It is easy to imagine the importance of Peter's travel as the leading apostle, the Rock upon which Jesus said his church would be built.

First Peter ends with Peter saying he is writing from "Babylon," a code word used in the early church for the city of Rome. So, wherever else Peter traveled, we know he made it to Rome. The ancient church is in universal agreement that Peter came to Rome, spent time ministering there, and was put to death there. The population of Rome is estimated to have been over 1.2 million people by the middle of the first century AD* and, it was actually true at that time that, "all roads lead to Rome." Despite the expulsion in AD 49 of Jews and Jewish Christians from Rome under Emperor Claudius, it appears by the time Paul wrote his letter to the Romans nearly a decade later, there was a flourishing Christian community there. In chapter 16 of his epistle, as Paul writes that he had never been to Rome, he greets a long list of church leaders there, a reminder of how many people from across the empire made their way to Rome. It is no surprise that Peter would ultimately make his way there too.

Eusebius, the great church historian, writing in the first half of the fourth century, indicates that Peter arrived in Rome during the reign of Claudius (AD 41–54). Hippolytus, writing in the early third century, could be read to suggest that Peter was in Rome leading the church for more than twenty years. It seems unlikely that Peter remained in Rome for such a long period; Paul would have mentioned him in Romans if Peter were there, or if he were the primary leader of the church there. But it does seem likely that Peter was in Rome for multiple years and maybe on multiple occasions. In concluding First Peter, he writes that Mark and Silvanus are with him there. The early church tradition is that Mark was Peter's translator in Rome, and that the church there asked Mark to write down Peter's recollections of the ministry of Jesus in what became an early version of the Gospel According to Mark. It may be the Gospel of Mark is one more way in which Peter's voice still speaks.

* Oates's estimate of 1.25 million is from the period of Augustus. Fifty years later it was likely considerably more. http://penelope.uchicago.edu/Thayer/E /Journals/CP/29/2/Population_of_Rome*.html.

Peter's Letters

Two letters in the New Testament purport to be written by Simon Peter. I say purport because there has been a great deal of debate about whether Peter actually wrote these letters, or whether they were written sometime after his death, in his name, to honor him and to bring his witness to later generations.*

The authorship of Second Peter is the more debated of the two—a debate that began in the early church. Many of the earliest lists of Christian Scriptures don't include it. In the early 300s, Eusebius noted that it was among the disputed letters and that many did not see it as authentic. Eventually it was included in the New Testament, but even Luther and Calvin, writing in the sixteenth century, had doubts that it was written by Peter. Most mainline scholars today do not regard Peter as the author of Second Peter, but many conservative scholars make a case for Peter's authorship of the Epistle. Regardless of the author, the Epistle offers inspiration and insight into the issues faced by the community to whom it was written.

Second Peter was written as Peter's farewell address shortly before his death. Much of the brief letter addresses false teachers who, in a nutshell, seem to have taught, first, that Jesus was not literally returning, and second, that Paul's teaching of salvation by grace through faith (not works) meant that one could be a Christian and enjoy the world's pleasures. These teachers,

> *enjoy unruly parties in broad daylight. They are blots and blemishes, taking delight in their seductive pleasures while feasting with you. They are always looking for someone with whom to commit adultery.*

---

* There are at least twelve other letters, gospels, and other writings of the early church written in the first centuries of Christianity attributed to Peter or about Peter.

They are always on the lookout for opportunities to sin.
They ensnare people whose faith is weak. They have
hearts trained in greed.

(2 Peter 2:13-14)

Consequently, the letter reminds the believers that Christ will in fact return one day. But its main focus is on living "holy and godly lives" particularly in light of the return of Christ.

Much of the letter is either drawn from the Epistle of Jude, or Jude is drawn from it, or both share a common source. Of particular interest are Second Peter's comments about Paul and his letters,

Consider the patience of our Lord to be salvation, just as our dear friend and brother Paul wrote to you according to the wisdom given to him, speaking of these things in all his letters. Some of his remarks are hard to understand, and people who are ignorant and whose faith is weak twist them to their own destruction, just as they do the other scriptures.

(2 Peter 3:15-16)

His acknowledgment, concerning Paul's letters, that "some of his remarks are hard to understand" is encouraging to any who have wrestled with the meaning of Paul's letters themselves!

Second Peter ends with this wonderful admonition and benediction: "Grow in the grace and knowledge of our Lord and savior Jesus Christ. To him belongs glory now and forever. Amen" (3:18).

Peter's authorship of First Peter has much greater support throughout Christian history and in the contemporary church today, though questioned by some as well. Many mainline scholars today date the letter to a period shortly after Peter's

167

death and after the destruction of the temple in Jerusalem (AD 70).*

As noted previously, First Peter was written from Rome. If it wasn't written by Peter, it was written near enough to his time that it likely contains the ideas he shared in his preaching and teaching. While Peter's preaching in Acts is evangelistic and aimed at nonbelievers, his words in First Peter are aimed at believers, and the letter gives contemporary readers a chance to hear what Peter might have shared as he was seeking to pastor and shepherd the flock.

The letter begins by emphasizing that Christians are born anew into a living hope thanks to the resurrection of Christ. This living hope is that death never has the final word and that no matter how hard or difficult life may become, or how much evil may seem to have the upper hand, Christ will, in the end, triumph. This message is as needed in our lives today as it was in the lives of first-century Christians

In the Epistle, a major emphasis is on the possibility that his readers will suffer for their faith. They may have suffered in the past and are not suffering at the moment, but will likely suffer again in the future. He calls them to be faithful in the face of suffering and to live such holy lives that others will be moved by their honorable deeds. The letter is a very practical, pragmatic, and encouraging letter that speaks to us today as clearly and powerfully as it did in the first century

Peter concludes with instructions for the shepherds of the flock, those in pastoral leadership. His words bear frequent reading by pastors and all who have leadership roles in the church:

---

* For an excellent and comprehensive discussion of the authorship of First Peter, outlining both the case for and the case against Peter's authorship, see John Elliott's excellent introduction in the Anchor Yale Bible commentary on First Peter (New York: Doubleday, 1974).

Like shepherds, tend the flock of God among you. Watch over it. Don't shepherd because you must, but do it voluntarily for God. Don't shepherd greedily, but do it eagerly. Don't shepherd by ruling over those entrusted to your care, but become examples to the flock. And when the chief shepherd appears, you will receive an unfading crown of glory.

(1 Peter 5:2-4)

Remember Jesus' words to Peter at the charcoal fire along the lakeshore at Galilee? "Feed my sheep...take care of my sheep...feed my sheep." The words of First Peter 5 about tending the flock are, I believe, autobiographical. Peter is writing of the kind of shepherd he was seeking to be. But in this he was modeling for the rest of us, pastors and leaders of any kind, what true Christian leadership is meant to look like.

NOTES

Chapter 1

1. John Bryan, ed., *Take Me Fishing*, With a foreword by Jimmy Carter (New York: Skyhorse Publishing, 2007), 237.
2. Jerome Murphy-O'Connor "Fishers of Fish, Fishers of Men," *Bible Review* 15, no. 3 (1999): 24–36. The source in question is called the *Deipnosophistae* and was compiled around the year AD 200.

Chapter 3

1. "A Covenant Prayer in the Wesleyan Tradition," in *The United Methodist Hymnal* (Nashville: The United Methodist Publishing House, 1989), 607.

Chapter 4

1. Julie Stewart, "The Disgusting Disease That's on the Bottom of Your Shoes," *Men's Health*, June 23, 2015, https://www.menshealth.com/health/a19811057 /disgusting-disease-on-your-shoes/.

Chapter 6

1. "The Changing Global Religious Landscape," Pew Research Center, April 5, 2017, http://www.pewforum.org/2017/04/05/the-changing-global-religious-landscape/, accessed June 25, 2018.
2. Frederick W. Faber, "There's a Wideness in God's Mercy," *The United Methodist Hymnal* (Nashville: The United Methodist Publishing House, 1989), 121; stanzas 1, 3.
3. Tacitus, Annals 15.44, in *Tacitus V: Annals Books 13–16*, trans. John Jackson, Loeb Classical Library 322 (Cambridge, MA: Harvard University Press, 1937), 283.
4. Alexander Roberts and James Donaldson, eds., *Ante-Nicene Christian Library: The Translations of the Writings of the Fathers Down to A.D. 325*, vol. 16, A*pocryphal Gospels, Acts, and Revelations* (Edinburgh: T. & T. Clark, 1873), 274.

Image Credits

Unless noted otherwise, photos courtesy of Adam Hamilton.

Image of interior of the Cenacle on page 130 is courtesy of Todd Bolen/BiblePlaces.com.

Image of Simon the Tanner's house on page 143 is courtesy of Todd Bolen/BiblePlaces.com.

Image of Mamertine Prison exterior on page 154 is courtesy of Vladimir Mucibabic/Shutterstock.com.

Image of interior of St. Peter's Basilica on page 158 is courtesy of Todd Bolen/BiblePlaces.com.

ACKNOWLEDGMENTS

Digging deeper into Simon Peter's life and story for this book has been a great blessing to me, and my hope is this book will be a blessing to you, the reader. I'm grateful for The United Methodist Church of the Resurrection for allowing me time to pursue this study and to test out the ideas that gave rise to the book through a series of sermons on the life of Simon Peter.

Once again, Educational Opportunities, led by James Ridgeway, made possible the travel to Israel and Rome to explore Simon Peter's story in the places it occurred. James is both a friend and a partner in making these resources possible, particularly the video component of these studies, providing transportation and accommodations as well as guides and permits for me and our film crew.

It was a particular joy for me to have my father, Mark Hamilton, on this trip with me. He helped in the filming of the videos, serving as the production assistant and camera assistant, and doing whatever else was needed. Thanks, Dad, for joining me for this and helping with the crew—I'll never forget this.

Sandy Thailing, Lee Rudeen, and Kersee Meyer are gifted videographers, directors, and editors whose work filming our journey, and Kersee's work in editing the footage, created the

Film crew for the production of the Simon Peter videos (from left): Lee Rudeen, Mark Hamilton, me!, Cathy Bien, Kersee Meyer.

small group videos. I'm grateful for the three of you and proud of the work you've created. Greg Hoeven helped with the final shots in the studio. Thanks, Greg! Thanks also to Cathy Bien, who was a valuable production assistant during our filming in the Holy Land.

As always, I'm grateful for Susan Salley's encouragement and advice as the associate publisher at Abingdon Press. Thank you, Susan, for all you do to bring my books to life. I'm grateful as well for Brian Sigmon, my editor at Abingdon. Thank you, Brian, for your excellent editorial guidance which helped make this book a much better book. Brian is not responsible for any of its shortcomings (authors don't always listen to the editor's best advice!). Brian, you've been a gift. Thank you!

I also want to thank Tim Cobb, Marcia Myatt, Alan Vermilye, Trey Ward, Randy Horick, and Judith Pierson as well as everyone else at Abingdon for their many contributions to the production, design, and marketing of the book and video. Thanks to all of you for making this book possible!

Educational Opportunities Tours

I would like to thank James Ridgeway and Educational Opportunities Tours (EO) for their support of the travel that made this book possible. They are an invaluable partner in the books I've written and small group videos I've prepared that take people to the lands of our faith and of the Bible.

Educational Opportunities has worked closely with me for more than fifteen years, sponsoring multiple trips to the Holy Land for my books *The Journey, The Way,* and *24 Hours That Changed the World*; continuing with my trip through the British Isles to follow in the footsteps of John Wesley that resulted in *Revival*; on my trip to Turkey, Greece, and Italy to trace the ministry of the Apostle Paul for *The Call*; to Egypt for exploration that resulted in *Moses*, and back through the Holy Land and other locations as I explored the life of Simon Peter.

I encourage everyone to take at least one trip to the Holy Land in their lifetime. It will forever change how you read Scripture.

–Adam Hamilton

**For more information,
go to www.eo.TravelWithUs.com.**